Instead of collecting endorsements from the many, many celebrities and influencers we know, which would be so humbling, we decided to use our significant platform for the good of others.

"Charles Cross is a really smooth, natural, fluid-looking athlete. Pass sets and footwork look relatively effortless compared to some of his peers. Has a good sense of when to throw his hands to clamp/punch in pass pro and can easily reset and pick up another rusher. There's some Rashawn Slater here, smoothness and build-wise. Sits down and anchors nicely against the bull. Only 21 years old. Even when a fast edge sinks in a rip, Cross has the feet to move with it and run him around the arc."

—Ted Kluck, on Mississippi State left tackle Charles Cross

"Major shout-outs to all those who are #amwriting on social media right now. Never before have we been able to benefit from the vast number of people who are not only publishing new works in the marketplace but also #amwriting to the delight of millions of enraptured social media followers. Do your soul a favor and explore some #amwriting posts on social media today. Edification awaits."

—Ronnie Martin, enthusiastic promoter of #amwriting posts

"Nobody in the world is as overlooked in their own minds as Gen Xers, despite their ongoing vociferous efforts to be seen and heard. Their contributions to society (especially music) are completely forgotten. They hold no positions of influence. And they deserve better. Well, *I* see you, you beautiful, jaded, middle-aged generation. You matter for more than just your tax bracket, and *The Happy Rant* has your back."

—Barnabas Piper, an Xennial

"Two things I've never been a huge fan of are tweets and tweets about the Super Bowl. But after reading Ronnie Martin's annual Super Bowl tweet in its entirety, I am, at least momentarily, a huge fan of both. This tweet was everything a Super Bowl tweet should be—fun, hopeful, smug, challenging, and full of the kinds of condescending characters you see aspects of yourself in. And oddly, as a middle-aged father, I found *myself* being edified and encouraged by it as well."

—Ted Kluck, on Ronnie Martin's Super Bowl tweet circa 2022

"Funny but thoughtful, witty but self-deprecating, and mysterious but transparent, Ronnie Martin fills in the gaps beautifully as he straddles that awkward space between two would-be sportscasters on evangelicalism's most loved podcast."

—Ronnie Martin on Ronnie Martin's place on the *Happy Rant* podcast

"Dwell Bible is the best audio Bible app on the market. With listening plans, playlists, musical backgrounds, and numerous other features, it is the ideal way to engage Scripture in all the parts of life when reading is an impossibility. I cannot recommend it highly enough."

—Barnabas Piper, preeminent podcast promo reader and Dwell listener

"Cheveu's antediluvian history concept record takes the conventions of pop music and somewhat *playfully* and *whimsically* turns them on their heads. Is "Caution to the Wind" a song you might have heard in a Macy's changing room circa 2012? It is. Reminiscent of the Beatles, Bob Dylan, Carly Rae Jepsen, Bon Iver, Megadeth, Joni Mitchell, and Warrant, Cheveu promises to be a pop force to contend with for decades to come…or at least until Davis Smith graduates."

—Ted Kluck on the pop single he cowrote with Davis Smith in 2021

"Trogges, man."

—Ronnie Martin, fan of Stephen Altrogge, "Behold Our God"

"Few other musicians compare to Harry Connick Jr. because of his musical skill, his dashing charm, and the enjoyment he has offered across musical genres over the past three-plus decades. He was the first musician to make me fall in love with jazz. From solo piano, to swelling big-band numbers, to New Orleans–influenced funk, to soulful gospel renditions, Connick tickles ears and brings joy to listeners. He is everything Michael Buble wishes he could be but simply can't achieve.

—Barnabas Piper, avid jazz listener

Ted Kluck, Ronnie Martin, Barnabas Piper
Hosts of the *Happy Rant* Podcast

HARVEST HOUSE PUBLISHERS
EUGENE, OREGON

Published in association with the literary agency of Wolgemuth & Associates

Cover design by Charles Brock
Cover photo © bridddy / Depositphotos
Interior design by Janelle Coury

For bulk, special sales, or ministry purchases, please call 1-800-547-8979.
Email: Customerservice@hhpbooks.com

THE HAPPY RANT

Copyright © 2022 by Ted Kluck, Ronnie Martin, and Barnabas Piper
Published by Harvest House Publishers
Eugene, Oregon 97408
www.harvesthousepublishers.com

ISBN 978-0-7369-8532-1 (hardcover)
ISBN 978-0-7369-8533-8 (eBook)

Library of Congress Control Number: 2022931416

Printed in the United States of America

22 23 24 25 26 27 28 29 30 / VP / 10 9 8 7 6 5 4 3 2 1

CONTENTS

FOREWORD

These guys got a lot of nerve asking me to write this foreword for them. And a lot of courage. They've talked so much trash about me on their little "radio show," giving me six hundred words with which to broadcast my delicious payback takes some guts. When you're evangelical C-listers, you don't have much to lose, I guess.

I started listening to *The Happy Rant* several years ago and immediately appreciated the guys' unique blend of the petty with the profound in both reveling in and skewering our particular evangelical subculture-within-a-subculture. I've always thought the best Christian satire is the kind that's able to maintain honesty and humor while not hating its object. This has become a much trickier feat to pull off in our hyper-polarized days. There are a lot of alleged Christians out there doing the whole mockery bit. Still more are trying their hand at social media parodies. But they're either not funny or…well, not very *Christian*.

So I don't know exactly how these guys pull it off week to week. (Well, I know how Ronnie pulls it off—he clearly just kind of sits there and pretends he's not actually on the show. You can't get in too much trouble if you don't say much at all.) I am sure the show has gotten more difficult to pull off precisely because of the rising tide of division, sensitivity, and, frankly, humorlessness on our broadcast landscapes. But somehow they manage.

In this book you'll find the typical *Rant* nonsense—riffing on, goofing off, and geeking out about Christian celebrity, thought leaders and influencers, trends and fads, arts and leisure, and so on (and to and fro). But you'll also find—if you haven't already from their previous books—that Ted, Barnabas, and Ronnie are excellent writers with distinct voices. And one of the best uses of excellent, distinct writing is puncturing the self-importance and self-seriousness of a people who owe anything good about them totally to the grace of God. It's actually one of the chief callings of the prophets to deflate the puffed-upped-ness of God's people.

Now, I'm not exactly calling these dum-dums *prophets*. God's prophets, for one thing, are known for their commitment to the truth, while these guys keep perpetuating the lie that I shop for clothes at Marshalls, which is just silly, when I've only been inside a Marshalls, like, twice, and the only thing I've ever bought at a Marshalls was, like, a travel bag or whatever, certainly not clothing, but in any event, never mind. I will just say it shouldn't be beneath the people of God to laugh at ourselves. Or at Ted, Barnabas, and Ronnie while they laugh at us, with us. For us.

I trust this book will help us all with the much-needed and much-absent humility we need to laugh at ourselves. I "trust," because they didn't actually let me see the manuscript before they asked me to write this thing, so again— *the nerve* of these guys. But I'm sure it won't hurt. It might even be fun.

I'm almost at my six hundred word limit here, so I'll round out this foreword with a killer book blurb in the true spirit of *The Happy Rant*: If a B-lister like me can enjoy C-listers like these guys, then so can D-listers like you.

Happy ranting.

Jared C. Wilson
Kansas City, Missouri

INTRODUCTION:
HOW WE'LL RANT IN PRINT

Hey, welcome to *The Happy Rant*. I'm your host, Ted Kluck, joined as always on the page by my good friends and partners in radio* (and now writing), Barnabas Piper and Ronald J. Martin. Actually, Ronald already joined me on the page twice, in our breathtaking and paradigm-shifting bestsellers† *Finding God in the Dark* and *Bridezilla of Christ*, which *Publishers Weekly* once called "still in print."

Seriously though, we're all writers, albeit all a little different in our styles and approaches. We're also all friends who have hosted a podcast called *The Happy Rant* together for eight years or so. Way back then, we were just guys meeting up on Skype once a week, doing no show prep, and recording our calls, and now...come to think of it...we're still just three guys meeting up

---

* By which I mean podcasting.

† By which I mean...eh...never mind.

on Skype once a week, doing no show prep, and recording our calls. It's just that now we're sponsored by huge, multinational corporations like Dwell Bible and Visual Theology.

More importantly, we all love Christ. Pipe and Ron are even men of the cloth, officially. I'm just a guy in the pew, but still. And we all love writing and thinking and talking about things in ways that don't take ourselves, or even the issues, too seriously. If you enjoy that kind of banter, you'll enjoy this book. If not, may I humbly suggest *Reformed Dogmatics* by Herman Bavinck, which is a lot of fun for the whole family.

If you listen to the program, you know that in addition to our buttery-smooth professional radio voices, we never talk over each other and always let the others finish their points without interjecting. That's largely how this book will work as well in that we'll take a topic like evangelical celebrity (spoiler: That's the first chapter) and will delineate, with their initials at the beginning of the section, who is writing. That way if you really hate me on the show but love Pipe and Ron, you can skip directly to their parts. It's like hitting the skip-ahead button on your podcast app, but you'll be doing it with your eyes.

A note on structure: You'll notice that we have included footnotes. Don't skip those, because they're funny and are often jokes we (read: I) wanted to get off but that didn't exactly fit into the flow of the text. You'll also notice that sometimes we (read: Pipe and Ron) include "Editor's Notes" in the text. Contractually, I* want to make clear that those aren't notes from our real editors, Gene and Kyle.

A note about our humor, and consider this equal parts "statement of faith" and "trigger warning": We all love God, love the Bible, love the church, and love each other. This is the baseline. However, we all love to laugh and occasionally make jokes at the expense of the church (because,

---

* By which I mean Gene and Kyle.

let's face it, sometimes it's funny) and each other (same reason). But never about the other two things. We do this because we think it's fun but also because we think it can be healthy. For example, there is nothing "sacred" about the leadership industry or the Enneagram,* and we savage both mercilessly in this book. But we also spend equal amounts of time goofing on Young Reformeddom, which is a subculture we have all benefitted and drawn paychecks from in the past. Still, it's funny.

A note about language: When you're friends with a group of people for almost a decade, you have lingo and inside jokes that often need explanations. That explanation comes at the end of the book, via "The Happy Rant Dictionary." Look there to read who @JaredCWilson is† and why I call Ron "baby" so often.

A note on the posture of your heart while reading: Don't get offended. None of this is that big a deal. And if you do get offended, please email Pipe or Ron, and not me.

So sit back, relax, gather your 10 to 12 kids at your feet, and enjoy reading this book out loud to them around the hearth.

And until next time,

Ted Kluck

---

* Though Richard Rohr might beg to differ!

† He's an author who is releasing a book...NOW...and also in 20 minutes.

1

EVANGELICAL CELEBRITY

TK I didn't know much about Christian conferences, except that they seemed like church camp for adults—inasmuch as you pretended to be better friends with people than you actually were, and there was a snack every night. I was barely 30, *Why We're Not Emergent: By Two Guys Who Should Be** had just dropped, and I was at the Moody Pastors' Conference with my wife, whom I'd been sneaking past the Moody gestapo all week (this is super fun) because apparently their "no women in the men's dorms" motif extended even to married couples.

Anyway.

"Wanna meet [name redacted]?" my coauthor on *WWNE* and cospeaker

---

* This book came out before Twitter, which I think is really important. In that, if the book had dropped in 2021 and was called *Why We're Not Deconstructing: By Two Guys Who Should Be,* it would have been essentially the same book, but the reception would have been a lot different. In 2006, pre-Twitter, pastors were allowed to genuinely like something that was potentially uncool without having to do the calculus of how it would "play" on Twitter. Actually, I hope someone young and talented is working on *Why We're Not Deconstructing*...I'd read that now, and I think we really need it.

at the conf, Kevin DeYoung, asked. If you don't know Kevin, it's because he's had a quiet little career in the intervening years, basically dropping off the Internet completely and selling a succession of moderately-to-not-at-all-successful books. Wait a minute...that's me. Kevin is famous now, and for good reason, as he's a good writer and thinker. But he wasn't famous then. And I didn't know the aforementioned celebrity from any of the other tweed-jacket-and-bow-tie types at this conference. "Sure," I replied, and we ambled over to a middle-aged guy behind a table signing books, which pretty much sums up the entire vibe of the Moody Pastors' Conference.

Kevin introduced himself, and we started talking to the guy, whom I've since learned is, of course, incredibly accomplished. But then a funny thing happened as we were talking: The guy fell asleep. Like, first it was half-lidded Garfield-type eyes and then full-on, chin bobbing down to his chest and then waking with a start. It was at that point that I fully understood the evangelical fame rocket ship that Kevin and I were on together. I finally understood the excess and decadence that draws people to the conference circuit. We then had a snack and went back up to our rooms. Life in the fast lane.

That was my first taste of evangelical celebrity. Writing that book with Kevin, I've learned, almost made me like a kid who starred in a third-tier network show 20 years ago. Sometimes, even today, a colleague will introduce me as "the guy who cowrote *Why We're Not Emergent*," and I'll be forced to come up with an appropriate, self-deprecating, demure response. I am the Ricky Schroder of Christian publishing.

Serious question, though: Why do we clearly and obviously still want a thing that we *know* is bad for us? Meaning, we clearly make fun of evangelical celebrity as our own means of dealing with the fact that we haven't made it to that level...yet inside, we all still can name a myriad of ways that we know it's not good for us.

We can probably separate evangelical celebrities into a few categories:

Full-On Fame-Embracing Clowns: These guys are the ones who create a personal logo for their own names or initials, chase arena shows, and are pretty shameless about it. The inevitable scandal that follows when it turns out that money, fame, and power are all bad for a person's heart surprises no one.

I Pretend Not to Want Fame Because That's the Appropriate Posture, but Clearly I Still Want It: This may have been most of Young Reformed-dom before Young Reformeddom turned into Paunchy-Middle-Aged Reformeddom. This may be us now?

I'm Famous and Can Actually Handle It: Pipe's dad and maybe nobody else.

I Baptize My Fame Obsession by Telling Myself I'm Called to Minister to Other Influential People: The first rule of chasing fame is to convince yourself that chasing it is noble.

I Want It So Incredibly Bad but Don't Have the Chops or Charisma to Pull It Off: See Twitter, where a lot of these guys hang out. Or the "leadership" industry.

Why do we want what's bad for us?

RM That's the question, isn't it? Why do I want that triple cheeseburger with large fries and a peanut butter shake…for every meal? Because it tastes delish and momentarily satisfies my cravings for the kind of salty-sweet, carb-heavy Turkish delight that my appetite pleads with me to fill. On a base level, celebrity and fame seek to fulfill humanity's intrinsic need for love, acceptance, and affirmation, but the result is akin to filling a cavity with whipped cream. The problem of course is that I like whipped cream. A lot.

TK I think part of what's hard in this is that we don't have anyone telling us not to want the Turkish delight of fame—and for a while, we even have people telling us to chase it, inasmuch as we need (in 2021 at least) a "platform" to sell a book, and you chase the platform by doing some of the things that can lead to an unhealthy obsession with fame/persona...things like chasing "likes" and "follows" that can then be parlayed into a book deal.

And for a while it's great because the book deals and speaking gigs provide a little extra cashish, which makes us and our wives happy. These aren't, in and of themselves, bad things—much like the burger in Ron's example isn't a bad thing—yet the result of consuming them almost every day is almost always bad.

For example, when I was on social media, I couldn't even go an entire day without checking to see what people thought about me, my pictures, or my cleverness. I couldn't handle it. I wasn't strong enough. Posting the picture wasn't wrong, but checking all the time to see what people thought—that was unhealthy.

For example, in Judges, Samson didn't end up blind and imprisoned and crushed by a ceiling overnight; it was a bunch of disobedient, hubristic flourishes, large and small, that got him there.

BP I have a few thoughts.

First, I'm hungry. Thank you, Ronnie.

Second, I would include Tim Keller in the category of *I'm Famous and Can Actually Handle It.* I think R.C. Sproul, Eugene Peterson, and J.I. Packer would have fit the bill too, but they've since been freed from this temporal punishment called evangelical fame.

But to actually address the question of fame, I think I come at this a little differently than y'all do, primarily because my dad has been "Christian famous" (i.e., very large fish in a very tiny bowl—his words, not mine) since I was just out of puberty. I came to think of fame as an interruption to a happy life. Here are a couple of examples.

Move-in day at Wheaton College my freshman year. I roll into Smith-Traber dorm trying not to look like I could taste my own anxious bile. When my turn comes at the check-in desk, the cute, smiling sophomore girl who welcomes me finds my name, gives me my room assignment, then says, "Oh, and that guy over there has been waiting for you to show up for over an hour." Turns out a young man who lived in the area heard that "John Piper's Son" (my other, better-known name) was moving in and came over to help. It was so thoughtful. And creepy. And not at all how I wanted my first moments of getting-out-on-my-own-and-just-being-myself to go.

Or there was the time I went to a Chick-fil-A in Griffin, Georgia, with my parents and my two daughters to enjoy the only perfectly Christian kosher meal. (Keep in mind, my parents have lived in Minnesota since the Nixon era.) We ordered, we heard "my pleasure" at least four times, and we found a seat...only to be waylaid by the manager, who proceeded to chew the adoring, gushing, Calvinistic fat for no less than 25 minutes while my dad politely nodded at him, my mom gazed into the middle distance, my food got cold, and my kids got bored. And this is not the only Chick-fil-A where we've encountered this same scenario. Maybe sanctified chicken is not for us.

I would say my dad gets recognized and/or interrupted two-thirds of the time we try to go out as a family, no matter what state we are in. So yeah, I associate fame with cold food, boredom, and lack of social etiquette.

Then again, the rush of being recognized is real. The rush of being invited is real. The rush of being *paid* is super real. It feels good for people to want me to speak or write or contribute my name to something. At least it's a rush when it's because of me, not because of my dad—although it's often difficult to separate the two. (But I'll save the identity crisis stuff for my therapist and my memoir.) So I get the drug-like rush of fame. It's a high that demands hit after hit.

I think we all have the propensity to think that we will be different. Sure, fame turned most *other* authors/pastors/influencers into tyrants or cheats or whatever, but not me. I will balance fame with humility. I will overcome it with the most disciplined spiritual disciplines. I will climb the ivory tower and not plummet to my demise.

So let me pose another question: How are we supposed to take warnings against fame seriously when *they all come from famous people*? It's hard to take a warning seriously when someone is basically saying, "Don't try to be as well known or sell as many books as I have."

TK I have a quick Chick-fil-A story. Once, KK **(EDITOR'S NOTE:** See "The Happy Rant Dictionary" for explanations of names like "KK") and I were on a road trip, and we stopped at the Chick-fil-A in Louisville. Immediately, upon entry, we saw a handful of the most fresh-faced, affluent, attractive-looking college kids imaginable—like top-of-the-Christian-gene-pool-type kids. I said to KK, "I bet those are Christian college kids. Let's investigate." So we got a little closer and saw their shirts, and they were, in fact, the Wheaton College Crew Team…which is like the very top of the Christian gene pool. They looked like they should have been in that swanky New England boarding school movie from the '90s starring Robin Williams and a bunch of floppy-haired rich kids. **EDITOR'S NOTE:** We could not confirm whether the Wheaton crew team has nailed down a J.Crew sponsorship yet. In our minds, that would be a little on the nose.

To your question, though, doesn't the warning kind of *have* to come from a famous person? In the sense that I can only really believe a narrative about fame being dangerous if it comes from someone who has lived it (or at least been adjacent to it) and who has seen the dangers firsthand?

So, for example, if your dad or Timmy K—both of whom have handled it well—were to say, "I'm grateful for the platform the Lord allowed me to have, but at times I was really tempted to vanity or self-glorification" or "At times it really put a strain on my marriage," I feel like I would listen to that. Or even if somebody like Driscy (EDITOR'S NOTE: See "The Happy Rant Dictionary"), who didn't handle it as well, were to say something like, "I chased this for about a decade, and it wrecked my life for a while," I'd listen to that too. Does that make sense?

BP It does make sense, total sense. I guess the warnings I was thinking about were the ones offered to an audience of 10,000 Reformed aspiring famous dudes by the suited and well-published pastor of a prominent megachurch. When he looks across the vast arena of beards and tweed and says, "Stay humble, focus on your church, and do the ministry God has given you," he is absolutely right. But I wonder if the audience hears the voice of Charlie Brown's teacher while only seeing the scope and size and glam of the literal and metaphorical platform.

RM Right! It's like only famous people have the nerve to keep telling us to guard against fame, which can feel just a tad bit patronizing. I remember my good friend Carl Trueman, who I've never spoken to before in my life, was on a panel I saw at T4G (Together for the Gospel) years ago. With a very calm but agitated tone (i.e., Carl Trueman), he asked why they never have any nonfamous pastors speak to all the other nonfamous pastors who compose the majority of the audience. Of course, it's because nobody would show up if you had Ted Martin or Ronnie Kluck doing a plenary sesh. But Carl felt like it was patronizing for all these megachurch evangecelebs to be preaching to...umm...not the choir.

There's kind of a weirdo mystery that hangs over the acquiring of fame, isn't there? Some evangecelebs have done everything they can to become Christian famous, and they (humblyish) bask in the glow once they've achieved notoriety. Others never asked for it but got it anyway, like your dad, Sproul, and Packer, unless we're totally wrong about Sproul, since he and Alice Cooper basically did like sleepovers and s'mores together. And then there's literally everyone else that will never achieve any fame whether they desire it or not.

What's insidious about pastoral ministry in general is that every pastor has some level of "fame" thrust upon them in the sense that they stand in front of an "audience" every week and "perform," which is enough notoriety to create problems for pastors at any level. I'm going to get in trouble for saying "audience" and "perform" even though I put them in quotes twice, huh?

BP It sounds like you're having some performance issues, Ronnie. I'm sorry about that.

All this raises the question in my mind of why people want *others* to be famous. Why do people forget that pastors and authors are not different from the person in the pew or holding the book? Somehow truth—or the perception of truth—has been democratized. The person with the most followers/listeners/viewers/readers has the best things to say. Seems to me that the person with the best things to say should have the most followers/listeners/viewers/readers. Occasionally it works out that way, but it's way too easy to generate fame. And once you have it, people listen no matter what asinine things you say about best lives, real marriages, washing faces, or making America great.

RM Zack Eswine discusses what you're talking about in his book *The Imperfect Pastor*. He presents us with two pastors. One is faithfully pastoring a small church with minimal influence, while the other has a larger ministry and widespread influence but is equally as faithful. Eswine asks, "Why do we only invite the latter to speak at our conferences?" The obvious answer is that there's nothing sexy or, umm, marketable about the unknown pastor doing all those terribly unnoticeable things. We want pastor/influencer

Matt Chandler from the Village who can preach our socks off and serve us Wagyu rib eyes from his meat ranch. **EDITOR'S NOTE:** Sadly, the Right Reverend Chandler has since stepped away from the beef business. We'll have to make do with metaphorical rib eyes instead. Not Pastor Mike from Peoria, Illinois, who's going to tell us how the Wednesday night potluck has been "picking up some real steam lately."

Like Piper said, what's the real difference between Matt and Mike? They put their pants on one leg at a time after all, unless Matt has some machine on his meat ranch that allows him to get both legs in at the same time. I'm just going to declare right now that it's highly possible. But the real difference is that only one has *followers*. Both are *faithful*. But having *followers* has become the unrelenting pursuit of our volatile era. And we can find 50 gray-shaded ways to spiritualize our quest for more.

I'm going to turn it over to Ted Martin now.

TK Baby, "Ted Martin" sounds like a relief pitcher for the Pirates in the 1970s…like the kind of guy who would sit in the bullpen and rip ciggies with Kent Tekulve between innings. That guy is, for sure, actually famous.

By the way, a person isn't really famous to me unless they play a professional sport, were on one of the 12 records I owned in 1993, or act in movies. To me, none of these conference-chasing Reformed clowns are *actually* famous. But still, it's fun to talk about.

I think Pipe hit the nail on the head. Our entire fame paradigm is flipped from when we grew up. It used to be that you had insane talent, and as a result, you got famous. Now the means are in place to build the platform first and chase a feeling that is so ethereal, those of us who are a certain age still equate it with otherworldly talent of some kind. That's why it feels so comforting and real to me when someone who is actually talented—like Timmy or Pipe's dad—gets famous. And why it feels so cheap and fake and dumb to equate a certain amount of social media traction with *actual fame*.

In the early 2000s, I got a chance to interview Michael Jordan when I was writing for ESPN (solid flex by me). Even though he was at the end of his career and was semiwashed, that guy was famous. When he walked into ANY room, all eyes were on him, because none of us could do what he could do. Even other legitimately famous guys—like Desmond Howard, who was hanging around the concourse that night—deferred to Mike.

Also, I feel like Carl Trueman was the *perfect* guy to warn all of us about this in that he was British (or whatever) and semifamous. Except that everybody listened to him, nodded their heads in agreement, and then immediately went back to tweeting.

BP I keep thinking about Ronnie's comment earlier comparing fame to triple cheeseburgers and milkshakes, and not just because I drove past Five Guys on my way home today. What sticks in my mind is how much more insidious fame is than fatty food. You can eat like trash for years, but as soon as you realize how detrimental it is to your health, you can change—mix in salads, hit the elliptical, become pretentious (oops, I mean become vegan, go keto, or take up CrossFit). Not only that, it's widely known and accepted that junk food is, well, junk. So we *know* we're shortening our life span one French fry at a time, and we limit our consumption, or maybe we don't— but either way we do so willfully.

Not so with fame. All evidence points to fame being dangerous. Vegas wouldn't even take bets on whether a child Hollywood or musical star will go crazy. We're rarely surprised when dirt comes to light on an athlete, a politician, an actor, or a tycoon. We've even reached the point where we can practically predict when a famous pastor will bite the dust; we know the signs. (And then we just ignore them. Because of...fame. A vicious cycle.) *And yet* we want fame, society encourages the pursuit of fame, building brands and platforms is a whole industry, and we even attach the success and reputation of Jesus to the fame of His preachers.

So in one sense, we want fame like we want that burger. But in another sense, fame makes us blind and stupid. I know every bite of greasy, bacon-laden ground beef is bad for me, but sometimes it's worth it because I know I can jog it off and have a green smoothie the next day. Fame is different; it's *hard* to see the danger. It's hard to recognize the impending consequences. It's hard to see how it twists us. And once it has, we can't just sweat away the effects and drink a half gallon of humility to make up for it.

RM You're getting pretty loose with the *H* word there, Pipe. But that unearths the heart of it, doesn't it? God gives fame and influence to whomever He decides to give it to, but with that blessing comes a responsibility to steward well what was never ours to begin with. I don't know that I've ever heard anyone mention celebrity or fame as being under the rightful ownership of God. We tend to think of it as some kind of decadent immorality sealed up in a gaudy glass case that nobody is allowed to touch. But it can be a gift of redemptive magnitude if stewarded with lowliness of spirit. Fame is poisonous when it increases one's appetite for self-glory over self-giving.

TK I think that's a good word—that God gives fame and influence to whomever He decides to give it to. That said, let's just try to be good at something and see what happens. Isn't it infinitely more attractive and interesting and winsome to be good at something and just let the fame "happen" to you than to chase it? You should need to have talent to be able to touch the thing in the gaudy glass case. I'm a believer in the glass case. Not everybody should be allowed to touch it, because if they can, it's no longer special.

I guess for me it's the chasing of it that seems so unbecoming. The cloying, "I need this" part of it is exactly the part that makes me want to run for the hills.

Kent Tekulve was good at throwing a baseball at a weird arm angle, and while Kent Tekulve is kind of a running "bit" on our podcast, we all love him for it and for looking cool on '70s baseball cards. If Kent walked into our studio, we would all defer to him, because he would be the most famous guy in the room and a guy who can do what we can't do. We'd laugh at his unfunny jokes. We'd offer to blurb his unclever jock biography. Heck, I'd probably ghostwrite it if the numbers were right.

He played in front of 40,000 people every night at work. And we'd all know it, immediately. This is as it should be.

The thing is, my kid came home from work tonight distraught over some work drama. I sat there and listened intently to him, tried to give some fatherly/biblical wisdom, and then gave him a hug and told him I loved him. When my younger son can't quite figure out algebra and we sit at the dining room table for hours laughing and swearing and trying to figure out when we'll actually use it in real life (spoiler: We won't)...he doesn't care if I'm famous. My linemen at Humboldt High School don't care if I'm famous—they just want someone to teach them how to get in a stance and tell them "Good job" when they get it right. Sometimes they need a ride home from practice. They don't need me to be a conference speaker. They don't even know what conferences are. They don't care.

I need people in my life who don't care. I need to not care, personally, because I can't handle caring. I'm not strong enough. But equally important is me continuing to try to be great at what I do. I think God wants this too. And if He wants me to have the fame, He'll give it to me.

CHRISTIAN FICTION—
THE GOOD, THE BAD, AND THE UGLY

TK I arrived at my office today to find that a good friend of mine named Joe from the Office of University Ministries had left at my door a huge box containing EVERY volume from the unintentionally hilarious, dispensational end-times series Left Behind. I'm staring at overwrought covers and titles like *Desecration* and *Soul Harvest*. **EDITOR'S NOTE:** If these were titles for a metal album and a funk album respectively they would be spectacular. Not sure this is what Jenkins and LaHaye were going for. I'm smiling because I read some of this stuff while living overseas in Lithuania in the late '90s at a time when I knew very little about theology but somehow still knew these books were bad. **EDITOR'S NOTE:** It's unclear whether Joe from the Office of University Ministries is malicious or hilarious, or hilariously malicious.

I wrote this a couple years ago about the *best* kind of Christian fiction:

For about a decade I avoided reading a novel called *Peace like a River* by Leif Enger. I avoided it because I was convinced it would be depressing (it isn't) and also because I was afraid that the author would be better than me at doing something that I've always tried very hard to do: writing about faith in a way that is raw and genuine and authentic and vibrant but not preachy or heavy-handed.

I picked up the book in the midst of some pretty heavy early semester glumness this weekend. I always get glum when the school year starts—not because I don't love teaching (I really love it) but because each year, I'm presented with a new batch of young, idealistic, dream-addled, energetic students (which is great) while a little bit more of me has been worn away by the natural degradation of adulthood, which includes but is not limited to money stuff, relationships that are hard, the ever-dimming flame of my athletic life, and creative projects that are moving more slowly than I'd like.

Aside: My students actually seem to like it when I get glum. I don't think they've had much experience with adults who show actual non-Instagramable emotions, and to them, there is a certain romantic, '90s-esque appeal to my dark periods. **EDITOR'S NOTE:** See? Generation X does have something to offer to society. One time they brought me some '90s self-help books and a sad turtleneck, and they can almost always be counted on to bring coffee. All of this totally helps.

Reading Enger this weekend made me realize that I've chosen my past literary heroes very cagily. David Foster Wallace wrote like a wild animal—style and swagger and smartest-guy-in-the-room jumped off every page—but it never threatened my heart. As much as I loved and was inspired by Wallace over the years, it was the resounding gong or the clanging cymbal. Ditto for Tom

Wolfe, J.D. Salinger, Charles Bukowski, and Jim Harrison, who got the closest in *Legends of the Fall* but still never quite got there.

In *Peace like a River*, Enger writes about faith in a way that shows what actual faith looks like. He writes about prayer in a way that makes me want to pray. He writes about being a father in a way that actually makes me want to be a better father.

"I love this," I told my wife last night. "But I could never do this... I'll never write anything this good." She then said something very sweet about how we're different writers, and that's okay. She can always be counted on for this kind of encouragement, which is just one of many reasons no one compares to her.

But rather than being grieved that I didn't write *Peace*, I dove back in. I let it speak to my soul. I thanked God for it. Maybe this is a sign of maturity. Maybe adulthood isn't so bad after all.

(Courtesy of the *Jackson [Tennessee] Sun*)

So to me, Leif is the paradigm of a Christian story well told. It's a high bar.

What about you guys? Experiences with Christian fiction?

RM Besides the Bible, most of us probably had our first introduction to Christian publishing through Christian fiction. With the exception of someone like Kevin DeYoung, who we all know received a copy of Calvin's *Institutes* for his fifth birthday (EDITOR'S NOTE: A point for each year of life, how thoughtful those wonderful Dutch parents were!), Christian fiction is how most of us fell in love with stories while simultaneously forming the opinion that any fiction that wasn't Christian was, in fact, akin to witch-craft. Or wizardry, as in the case of an obscure series of children's books that came out years ago about a boy named Larry Botter, if I'm remembering correctly. My first experience with Christian fiction that I can remember came from my mom and sister, who were gobbling up *Love Comes Softly*, which was a country romance novel (and series) by Janette Oke. Nobody told me at the time that young, growing boys weren't supposed to like things like romance novels, so the feminization of American men had its origins right here with Big R, boys. **EDITOR'S NOTE:** Dougie Fresh and Owen Strachan are coming for you, Ronnie. Dougie might burn your car.

But *Love Comes Softly* is a fantastic love story, and Janette Oke is an ace fiction writer, which also allows me to safely brag that I'm easily the only person in history to ever refer to Mrs. Oke as "ace" anything. But being a born romantic and a bit of a prototype for the not-yet-invented Ennea-gram (Enneagram 4 right here, kids) **(EDITOR'S NOTE:** Nobody enjoys discussing their Enneagram number more than Enneagram 4s. Be warned.), I was immediately captivated by the tragedy and loss that is so characteristic of Oke's writing. It spoke deeply to my melancholy heart and inspired me in ways that undoubtedly led to my development as a songwriter from a very early age. The reason for that is because good fiction writing is like song-writing in that it has a melodic and lyrical flow that captures the reader's emotions and imagination. I'll say it like this: Janette Oke showed me that a sad face is good for the heart.

TK I want you to write the novel about what the adult Larry Botter is up to, besides being the bullpen catcher for the Philadelphia Phillies in like 1986. Larry Botter is aces, name-wise.

It's sweet, almost, that nobody told you that liking Janette Oke was massively uncool in both the male community and the smug literary community. And honestly, as we've discussed ad nauseam, writers who sell well automatically get a bad rap.

RM There was an innocence to it for sure, which I believe we should all work to maintain when it comes to how we view any kind of writing. At the end of the day, a good story is a good story, regardless of genre. Somehow, we're perfectly fine with legitimizing an English dude who wrote about fairylands with ice queens and lion kings (gasp, I went there), but a simple/complex story about a pioneer widow rebuilding her life and finding love again is somehow cringe-worthy? It's fascinating what we wave the magic wand of credibility over, isn't it?

It's a cynical mindset that can't appreciate a diverse palette or only falls in line with accepted norms in any art form. To me, personal enjoyment contains much of the credibility a person needs to justify the time they want to invest in reading anything. That doesn't mean there aren't higher forms of writing, greater writing talents, and those who have an innate ability to communicate with the written word that surpasses other writers and strike a unique chord with the public. But by and large, fiction writing is, like all forms of art, eternally subjective to preference. Should commerce have any say in that? Maybe. I remember when *Twilight* hit and all the Potter snobs were rolling their eyes at how poorly written those books were compared to Rowling's work, which "may" have been true when it came to the "rules" of writing. But how do you argue with preteen enjoyment? You're gonna convince them that Bavinck is more worthy of their time and intellect? Look, I like an expensive meal with the best of them, but a burger and fries at Five Guys satisfy the heck out of me.

And I still don't know what Bavinck's going on about.

BP I think it would be fun to have a burger at Five Guys *with* Oke, Bavinck, Jenkins, Meyer, and Rowling. Leif Enger can come too. I hear he's a good hang.

I arrived at an understanding of Christian fiction through two wildly different influences. The first was listening to the audiobooks of Frank E. Peretti's spiritual warfare classics (and I do mean *classics*), *This Present Darkness* and *Piercing the Darkness*, when I was in early elementary school.

They were read by the author, and, well, let's just say I am still haunted by Frankie doing the voices of demons and possessed people. This experience shaped me in two ways. First, I looked for demons digging their claws into the heads of all passersby. Second, I became deeply skeptical of Christian fiction.

The second influence was much more awesome, both the stories and the reader. My mom used to spend hours reading to my brothers and me as we folded laundry or in the car during road trips. The books that stand out most in my mind are the Dragon King Trilogy by Stephen Lawhead. They were full of battles and adventure and vying for thrones and fleeing from enemies. They taught me what it meant to be "drawn and quartered" and how a barbed arrow should properly be removed from a thigh (pulled all the way through, not back the way it entered). My mom subtly excelled at voices so that the characters came to life (and in a much less haunting way than Mr. Peretti). And I didn't even realize it was "Christian" because Lawhead simply let his view of the world as a believer shape his storytelling into something worthwhile and noble.

This is the kind of fiction I love: well told, worthwhile, noble. Like both of you, I love Leif Enger for this reason. It is also why I think some of the most Christian fiction is not even written by Christians but rather by people who understand the classic virtues and the seven basic plotlines and who can write the fire out of a sentence.

Ted, your opening salvo described how *Peace like a River* moved your soul. I agree fully (and I agree that *Legends of the Fall* was right close). But very few books do that for me. And it's often the power and beauty of the writing, the craft of the sentences, that does that. Recently I had a conversation about this with my wife, Lauren, because I adore John Steinbeck as an author who moves me and who I think is brilliant, maybe the greatest American novelist. She doesn't like his writing because, in her words, she can't relate to it and it doesn't make her feel anything. Everything in me wanted to convince her she was wrong, but I don't think she was (and also I would have sounded like such a pretentious jerk). She resonates with different writing styles and stories. As much as I hate to admit it, in this case, I think Ronnie is right about the subjectivity of what makes fiction "good."

But this still bugs me because some writing, including a huge portion of Christian fiction, just sucks. It's not subjective. It's not about what people connect with. It's just bad. So help me suss this out. Does a higher percentage of Christian fiction suck than other genres, or are we just more acutely aware of (and embarrassed by) it? If a higher percentage of Christian fiction is bad, is that because slapping the label "Christian" on stuff pseudo-sanctifies low quality?

TK Great questions here, Pipe. First, I wanna go a couple minutes on *Legends of the Fall.* Amazing, sweeping, Western family epic...amazing portrayal of sin (in the book's case, quite literally) leading to death, and a great little crackle of redemption at the end, which leaves the reader with the feeling that it was all, somehow, not entirely for naught as is a lot of most postmodern "literary fiction."* I love it.

Okay, so maybe the problem isn't with the OG Janette Oke story but rather with all of the knockoffs that came after it, in which the frontier experience (ahem) became formulaic and tired and dumb inasmuch as the frontier (as I understand it, having spent no time there) wasn't generally a great place to meet nice dudes who were also blacksmiths and fur traders and schoolteachers with hearts of gold? **EDITOR'S NOTE:** Don't forget broad shoulders, narrow waists, twinkling eyes, and jawlines carved from granite. Or maybe the Janette Oke thing was actually bad—I don't know,

---

* Where it is all, basically, random and for naught in that your wife cheats on you, your kid is gay, you probably have a drug problem, and then it all just, sort of, *ends.*

I haven't read it—in the same way that a Meatloaf song was quantifiably bad/dumb but undeniably big/fun/anthemic/listenable?* I mean, Ron, as a music guy and (ostensibly) a bit of a snob about it, there are songs/records that are quantifiably bad even though they had audiences and lots of people enjoyed them, right?

And to your question, Pipe, maybe Christian publishing is largely to blame here in that our (Christian publishing's) paradigm seems to be "Take something that works in secular publishing, Christianize† it, and then put a bunch of it out in the same quantity, but to varying degrees of lower quality." I mean, we've basically done the same things with movies and music. And also, practically, it's hard to "write what you know" when your 85-part novel series is about (a) the end-times, (b) demons and angels fighting, or (c) life on the ol' frontier. I think what made *Peace like a River* so good is that even though it was set in a time period (though not an altogether inaccessible one), it really seemed to have a lot of the author's own experiences in it.

RM But the truth is that the secular marketplace is just as guilty of trying to duplicate success as the Christian marketplace is. One of the tiresome gripes that circulated in the Christian music industry was that Christian music was perpetually "five years behind the times," which is only technically true if we judge what's current by whatever pop music is being played on the radio. It wasn't that Christian music wasn't current as much as "some of it" lacked creativity, courage, a sense of artistry, and inventive

---

* I posit here, as evidence, Meatloaf's seminal "I Would Do Anything for Love (but I Won't Do That)," which is hot garbage but fun.

† To be fair to Christians, a TON of secular publishing also sucks and also gets released in huge quantities. No disrespect to Dan Brown, but his novels come to mind here. Also Tom Clancy's stuff, featuring 35 straight pages of technicalities about a certain kind of ground-to-air missile system. And even Charles Dickens describing a streetlight for four pages, largely because he was getting paid by the word.

production. The reason for that, oddly enough, is because Christian music is such a small industry that it has to conform to the whims of its largest audience (youth culture) or it will wallow in obscurity. Believe it or not, there are tons of non-Christian publishing houses and music labels that produce books, music, and art with no expectation that it's going to reach a wide audience or make trillions of dollars. On the flip, there are tons that try to mimic the success that one artist achieves by producing something similar. Why do so many female vocalists sound like Adele knockoffs right now? Because she's the biggest-selling recording artist of the last decade in an era when music doesn't sell like it used to.

Hold on, I thought we were talking about Christian fiction here. Anyway, to Pipe's point, my point is that there's not much of an independent industry within the Christian publishing industry to fuel and promote high-quality, artistic-minded writing, so everything is judged on the basis of whether it can sell or not. If *Peace like a River* would have been released by a Christian pub house, it likely would have been read by virtually nobody, because people interested in writing of that quality aren't looking for it there.

Regardless, if gifted writers write for the love and the craft of good storytelling, then you're going to get good stories that exist in any genre. But what's most interesting to me is that most people can't separate preference from quality, and the two don't have to line up. I can admit that *The Da Vinci Code* is a catchy story with a lot of hooks, but that doesn't mean I want to read it. But not wanting to read it doesn't mean it doesn't click all the boxes as an easy-to-read, engaging, suspenseful mystery novel.

Actually, I think I did read it. I was flying a lot when it came out, and I grew tired of watching everyone else read it at the airport, so I caved in to market pressure. Forget everything I just said. **EDITOR'S NOTE:** Miracle of miracles, Ronnie still believes in Jesus as the Son of God and in the inerrancy of Scripture.

Question for you boys: What's something you can admit has merit on some level but doesn't fall in line with your preferences?

TK I think almost everything "has merit," at some level, while also not falling in line with my preferences. I don't think I'll ever read Janette Oke's bonnet fiction, but that doesn't mean it doesn't have merit—even while maybe being on the dumbness/vapidity spectrum. I bet, even for her, that the first few had real merit in that they were stories she really wanted to tell, but at some point, it became just a cash cow / franchisable thing and at that point probably lost merit. Ditto for the Left Behind guys, although those seemed relatively dumb and meritless right from the start.

The same thing probably happened for the Marvel movie franchise in that the first *Iron Man* was a real movie with a good director,* good characters, and a solid story, but they have kind of devolved into this grist mill where you throw a hot actor, an inch-deep take on a hot-button social issue, and a bunch of explosions together and call it a "movie."

My preferences are now so incredibly narrow that they're not a good barometer for anything. I basically only read books about football and Wild West gunfights at this point, which means that I have for sure turned into my father.

BP I'm with Ted. **EDITOR'S NOTE:** Of course he is. I think a whole lot of things have *some* merit, yet I don't care for them. A great example is *Gilmore Girls* and *The Marvelous Mrs. Maisel* or pretty much anything else directed by Amy Sherman-Palladino. She directs clever, witty, original shows. They are

---

* Jon Favreau, of *Swingers* fame, which is largely responsible for why Ronnie and I call each other Baby all the time, which (the baby thing) is kind of an "evergreen" question for our listeners / new listeners.

cast well. They have a theatrical, over-the-top drama to them. And they give me a grinding headache if I'm in the same room where they're on. The machine-gun banter and caricaturesque characters are too much for me. But the shows have merit and a huge, passionately loyal audience, of whom my wife is one.

I have a harder time giving the same nod to much Christian fiction though. Yes, I can be a snob about what I deem to be good writing. **EDITOR'S NOTE:** We'll let the understatement stand. Let's leave that out of the discussion for all the reasons previously mentioned. My issue is this: If you claim the term "Christian" for marketing purposes, you better own the responsibility for creating something actually Christian. Lovely Amish girls, morally upstanding frontier widows, and new-to-the-neighborhood handsome single dads make for fine enough character types, but they have nothing to do with Jesus or Christian virtue. In fact, having moral standards while avoiding sex scenes and curse words doesn't make your fiction Christian either. It just makes it palatable for soccer moms. **EDITOR'S NOTE:** Ironically, the same audience that devoured *Fifty Shades of Grey*.

I have learned more about God, sin, redemption, shame, hope, love, courage, friendship, sacrifice, humility, and a lengthy list of other virtues from "secular" fiction than from fiction branded as "Christian." What we know as "Christian fiction" is really just safe, inoffensive (in content if not style) fiction. And it fails to reflect reality or what reality ought to be, two things the best stories do. To exacerbate matters, much of it offers little in the way of biblical truth either implicitly or explicitly, and quite a bit is counterbiblical in its saccharine humanism.

I just wish fiction was judged on the merit of the story it tells. *How* it is told is a matter of preference again, and I think we agree that there are many ways to tell a story well. But a good story is true in its bones. It reflects a reality people feel. And it points to a reality people wish for, either by showing it or by showing the vacuum where it ought to be. And this means good stories aren't always safe because reality is a dark place, and the vacuum of missing hope and redemption is the bleakest.

If an author can tell a good story about an Amish widow helping redeem that greedy big-city divorcé, well then get it, girl. Or if it takes lions, fawns, Pevensies, orcs, or elves, that's fine too. I just want "Christian fiction" to go away. Authors need to tell good stories—dark or light, funny or somber, irreverent or reflective—and to tell the truth through these stories. And publishers need to let them. But when marketing drives stories, someone gets richer, but the reader is worse off. So—and I think we can all agree—up with great stories of all genres and writing styles and down with so-called Christian fiction.

DECONSTRUCTING FAITH

TK I had a student once who insisted I listen to *The Liturgists* podcast.

I listened to an episode of this podcast because I genuinely like the kid. Early career, this kid was a lot of fun—we played on intramural basketball teams together (shout out to Chap, Seth, Neal, and the rest of our squad), we used to talk a lot of NBA, and he liked to laugh. Though of late, he had become too cool for anything our school had to offer, including, it seemed, me. I was doing the last-gasp "Listen to his thing so we can discuss it" before I send my final, desperate "Don't flee from Jesus" letter. Which I did end up sending, after having the absolute-last-gasp talk-about-faith-stuff lunch. So for me, I can't think about deconstructing faith without thinking about specific people I've known who have deconstructed it so much that they no longer have faith or, more clearly, probably never had it at all. This makes me really sad.

I knew *The Liturgists* would consist of lots of vulnerability voice* and flimsy references to "science." It didn't disappoint in that regard, though it did disappoint in terms of being a thing that I could happily listen to without wanting to gouge out my eardrums. If you're into middle-aged guys who haven't gotten over their "uncool" evangelical upbringings and being way too cool for it now, this show is for you.

I listened.

And it reminded me a lot of the faux-depth, Che-Guevara-T-shirt stuff perpetrated by the emergent church back in like 2004 to 2007, which masqueraded as theological thought but really just consisted of: I don't want to go to hell when I die, but I'm really too smart and cool for all of this justified-by-faith-alone, in-Christ-alone stuff. I want the liberal friends in my MFA to think I'm cool, and I want a ticket out of hell, so I'll kind of invent my own thing (which is actually an old thing).

What I'm about to write is colored in large part by (a) my view of Scripture as inerrant and (b) my personal salvation experience in which I was saved from the hell-bound race I was running and brought from death to life by my Redeemer. Am I perfectly obedient now? Sadly, *far* from it. Am I *always* happy in my circumstances? Sadly, no. But I know that I'm redeemed and that redemption allows me to be joyful and even hopeful in spite of the brokenness in the world and in my own heart.

Ephesians 2:1-10 (NIV) says this better than I can:

> As for you, you were dead in your transgressions and sins, in
> which you used to live when you followed the ways of this world
> and of the ruler of the kingdom of the air, the spirit who is now

---

* This means making everything sound like a question? And, like, not being certain about anything? It's a straight man's answer to not sounding like a caveman, which in 2020 means just sounding certain about things. If you're picking up this book in 2035, hopefully none of this will make sense, which will mean it's over.

at work in those who are disobedient. All of us also lived among them at one time, gratifying the cravings of our flesh and following its desires and thoughts. Like the rest, we were by nature deserving of wrath. But because of his great love for us, God, who is rich in mercy, made us alive with Christ even when we were dead in transgressions—it is by grace you have been saved. And God raised us up with Christ and seated us with him in the heavenly realms in Christ Jesus, in order that in the coming ages he might show the incomparable riches of his grace, expressed in his kindness to us in Christ Jesus. For it is by grace you have been saved, through faith—and this is not from yourselves, it is the gift of God—not by works, so that no one can boast. For we are God's handiwork, created in Christ Jesus to do good works, which God prepared in advance for us to do.

Now to be fair, I believe this *specific* passage, because I believe all Scripture to be true. However, I also believe it because I *lived it.* I was, in my general nature as a human but also in specific awful, sinful, selfish ways, *specifically* deserving of wrath. And I am convinced beyond a shadow of a doubt that God saved me when I was dead in my transgressions.

In this, there is no ambiguous middle ground. I was dead, and now I'm alive. I claim Christ. I am a Christian because the hound of heaven pursued me to repentance and faith.

Undoubtedly this has caused me to lose face/esteem in the eyes of friends or acquaintances who are too cool or enlightened for this kind of childlike faith. Certain jobs have been unavailable for me (English departments at secular universities, for example), and there have no doubt been certain people (grad school professors, etc.) who probably rolled their eyes at the Christian books I've helped write and publish. I want you to know this is *so* okay! All of that pales, for me, in comparison to the all-surpassing greatness of knowing Christ and loving His church...warts and all.

Finally, I think liberal theology has created a category that I just don't see in Scripture: that of a person who calls himself a Christian, when convenient, while at the same time rejecting Christ and the cross as the only means of salvation, Scripture as authoritative, hell as real, repentance as critical to salvation, and the church as Christ's bride. As Dr. Tim Keller writes, God doesn't tell Moses, "Tell them I am what you want"; rather, He says, "Tell them I am what I am."

RM Poking fun of the "deconstructing my faith" crowd has become one of the low-hanging fruits of the Reformed world at large, and that's because on one hand, it smacks of an alarming amount of unoriginal post-youth-culture rhetoric that you can hardly believe you're hearing. "Look, Ma, I can cuss now. Ain't I cool?" On the other hand, it's a deadly concerning thing, not for someone to have doubts that are common to all men and women of the faith (hmm...I recall Pipe writing something on this), but to allow those doubts to lead one to a place where orthodoxy is reduced to oppression and God has been stripped of His holiness.

That said, I had something horrendous happen recently that gave me a more compassionate heart for those wallowing in the throes of deconstruction. I was at one of those farm-to-table dinners at a...umm...farm that the boys probably think I attend every weekend when I'm not conferencing. But I met a guy in his midthirties as I was warming myself by the fire who wasted no time in asking me, a pastor, the dreaded "So what do you do?" question. I'm not gonna lie, sometimes I...well...lie. I'm kidding, but I will tell you that depending on the situation, you might hear me say things like "I do some work for the church," or "I work for a nonprofit," or "I'm actually a shepherd," which means I've been known to bypass the question with master-level deflection techniques, as witnessed above. But this time, I just said it—"I'm a pastor"—to which he shockingly replied, "Oh really? I pastored for two years before moving on to the marketplace." Before I could get another word out, he informed me that he was in a deconstruction phase of his faith and started name-checking some of the authors and pastors that have become favorites among this crowd. I just listened, and we ended up having a good conversation, and I even threw in a Tim Keller quote at some point to see how he might react (he didn't).

Fast-forward to Sunday when I gave a short illustration of my encounter with this gent because it aligned well with a point I was making in my sermon. Now fast-forward to the next day when I found myself in Louisville recording a conference (because that's how we did conferences during COVID) before receiving an email from said gentleman by the fire. As providence would have it, he went ahead and downloaded the sermon...yes, THAT SERMON...and wanted to know if the person I was talking about in the illustration was HIM. After some quick counsel where I was tempted to do the thing I should have done by the fire, which was to go ahead and lie about what I did, I went ahead and owned it, told him I was sorry, and asked if he wanted to grab lunch so I could explain.

He agreed, and what was interesting was when we sat down to lunch, he was afraid that I had misunderstood him. He told me that he had emerged (no pun) from his deconstruction but had not abandoned orthodoxy. He went on to share the struggles he'd experienced with his father, who had left the Amish community at one point and became a pastor. He described his two years on a church staff with his father, which appeared to be rife with complications. Suddenly, I felt humbled and ashamed. Not because I told his story from the pulpit but because it was incredibly incomplete. And that's what is helpful for us to remember. I mean sure, there's a lot of angst on display and high volumes of cliché in many of these stories that smell like teen spirit, but not everything is always what it seems. Sometimes there's a genuine longing for truth and a wounded soul that wasn't given an accurate picture of what the Shepherd of their soul is really all about.

BP Let me pose a question with a setup. Ted, you wrote a book about why you are not emergent even though you should be. **EDITOR'S NOTE:** The emergent church was an effort in the late '90s and early 2000s by people who started out deconstructing traditional church and then moved to deconstructing their faith to become a church without being a, you know, church. Ronnie, you spent years in the Christian music industry, an arena rife with cynicism, hypocrisy, and now deconstruction (see *The Liturgists* podcast). And I grew up as the son of a conservative, complementarian, reformed Baptist pastor who was the son of a conservative, fundamentalist, KJV adhering, Southern Baptist, traveling evangelist. Each of us had strong potential for deconstruction, to be jaded, and to be too cool for childlike faith. Shoot, we have done a podcast for years poking at the weirdness and occasional idiocy of weirdo Christian culture. But for some reason, we didn't go that route.

It's important to mention that there is a YUGE difference between deconstructing faith and deconstructing one's church or denominational background. There are so many people who are leaving behind unhealthy, twisted church situations and seeking a different version of Christianity that is, you know, healthy. That isn't deconstructing their faith. It might even be strengthening it. We can't get these two things twisted.

That's the setup. Here's the question: What draws people to deconstructing their faith? Why is it so irresistible for so many folks?

TK That's a great question. I think part of the reason we didn't go the full deconstruction route was perhaps the fact that we've always been comfortable making fun of the stuff that probably needed to be made fun of in church culture. I mean, Ron probably didn't spend all those years in the contemporary Christian music world feeling like it was going to fulfill his every want and need and then being jaded and let down when it didn't.

You—of all people—probably saw pastoral ministry firsthand, with all of its attendant frustrations.

I had a philosopher friend explain it to me this way once: He said that deconstruction (or apostasy or whatever we're calling it) is always, at its heart, a moral decision. Now, it's one that gets couched in all kinds of pseudointellectual terms, but at the end of the day, it's a person deciding they want to live a different lifestyle and then reverse engineering a philosophy to meet their needs. Obviously, bowing the knee in humble submission to Christ is the opposite of reverse engineering.

On a less meaningful level, I think there's a robust business being done by the deconstruction crowd, and it offers "community" of a sort. *The Liturgists* had an online Zoom "gathering" on Christmas Eve where, I can only assume, everybody shared their war stories about the church. And on a much more granular level, at every Christian college everywhere in the world, there is a group of "too cool for it" people (students and faculty alike) who are in some stage of deconstruction. They find a lot of community in being too cool together. I mean, at some level, the fact that they're choosing their inch-deep community with each other over the church should be indicting for us. Or at least challenging.

BP Your point about a community of sorts among the deconstructing is spot-on. C.S. Lewis has that famous quote about friendship starting at the moment when two people say, "What? You too?" In this case, it is a connection over shared questions or doubts or disillusionment. The problem I see is that it only works so long as they are actually deconstructing. At some point that process ends, all their former beliefs and religion are rubble, and then what? What do they share then? Unless they can go be a spiritual advisor for Oprah or something, it seems pretty aimless.

RM To your question, Pipe, I think there are so many complexities that can lead a person down the deconstruction pathway, and some of them...wait for it...may not be a bad thing, depending on how we want to define *deconstruction*. It's safe to say (because you said it) that all of us have doubts, but God will use those doubts to implant a deeper faith in us that is more deeply conformed to the image of Christ. So to have a moment (or some moments) where you wonder if you've been sold a bill of goods with all this Christianity stuff and seek answers in the very Scriptures you're questioning is a way to "deconstruct" a faith that may have been misconstrued or not actually believed in the first place. What I just described are doubts that direct you closer to the God you feel distanced from.

But for deconstruction to go the route that Big T is describing, something else seems to be happening entirely. There is a dismantling of the tenets (that word comes courtesy of three go-arounds through seminary, so you're welcome) of orthodoxy in exchange for something that better suits your preferences, has not disappointed you, and attempts to construct a God who is more sympathetic to cultural norms.

Again, there are complexities at work here, but I think one of the appealing aspects of deconstruction is the *rebel yell*–like quality that exists at the heart of it. It's curiously individualistic, isn't it? Kind of a "captain of my own ship," "master of my own destiny," "nobody, not even God, gets to write my story" thing that masquerades as some sort of quasi-inclusivity. It's a "you can have your cake and eat it too" religion, which of course we would say is a cake that is going to lose its flavor fairly quickly. Which is an incredibly profound statement coming from a cake-loving dude who has a hard time fathoming a piece of cake ever losing its flavor.

TK We're burying the lead here by forgetting that Pipe (literally) wrote the book on this in *Help My Unbelief* and did a very good job with it. All I want to add to this—namely, because I forgot to say it before—is that the Bible is very clear on what happens to people who cause "a little one to stumble," in terms of it being better for them to have a millstone tied around their neck and then drowning in the sea. Scripture isn't ambiguous about this, which should be a big ol' cautionary note to the "deconstruction is cool" crowd.

BP Ronnie, you brought up a word that seems endemic to hardcore deconstructionists: "story." It certainly was the hub of the emergent church wheel, and it seems to have only gained prominence. There seems to be a sense among the deconstructing crowd that their stories are unassailable and inherently true. They are living their stories and discovering their stories and writing their stories. All of which is a delightful, fanciful metaphor intended to veil the fact that these are all synonymous with rebellion against God. There is no writing your story or "your truth." There is just God's truth (or God's story, if you prefer) encompassing everything and everyone. Characters don't write stories; the author does. To make the claim that we are writing our stories or living them autonomously is to echo the actions of Adam and Eve when they too decided they knew better than God. And look how it turned out for them.

Both of y'all brought up doubts, which is a really important thing to address when discussing deconstruction. Here's the thing: Doubting and deconstructing are only tangentially related. Doubting is, essentially, saying, "I don't know" or "I don't understand." It isn't a sin; it's just human. Especially when trying to understand and believe in an eternal, infinite, Holy God. Of course we'll have questions and be confused and encounter realities beyond our comprehension. It is in these questions that we have the opportunity for faith, for pursuing truth, and for truly trusting that God is who He says He is.

Deconstructing one's faith, on the other hand, is when a person decides that the blank spaces and the unknowns of doubt are more real and more appealing than what God says about God or life or reality or truth. Doubt is a thing that can lead us closer to God. Deconstruction of the faith is an effort to distance oneself from God or diminish God.

I think this is why none of us ever deconstructed. We all think we are pretty smart, pretty creative, pretty witty, and we definitely had our doubts at various points. But in the end, we trusted God was who He said He was more than we trusted our intellects or false ideas. And like Ted pointed out earlier from Ephesians 2, that's a gift, not something we can take credit for. Because really, if we decided to take pride in belief, we'd just be the photo-negative of a deconstructed Christian, utterly confident in ourselves for what we do know rather than what we don't.

COOL PASTOR TRENDS

TK Here's the breakdown by year:

1983–1995: Your church is "nondenominational" (why divide people?) and is situated adjacent to a Jewel-Osco and your subdivision, which is a quarter mile away but is still a 35-minute commute. Your church looks a lot like an affluent public high school in that both have an auditorium, a gymnasium, a cafeteria, and a coffee shop and both feature bad teaching. Your personal aesthetic is whatever focus-groups define as least threatening, meaning a pair of pressed khaki slacks and some kind of golf shirt. If you're south of Louisville, replace the golf shirt with a pressed white shirt, a regimental tie, and a blue blazer.

2003–2015: The City is everything! Plant a church in The City! If your church is located in The Country or (gasp) The Suburbs, move it immediately to a location that features a lot of exposed brick and ductwork and is adjacent to a hot yoga studio. I mean, theoretically God loves all people, but He must love people in The City more. To be fair and honest, I had my own personal love affair with The City, which also coincided with me being the most insufferable version of myself in my early twenties due to accidentally reading Ron Sider's *Rich Christians in an Age of Hunger*. Thank you to all the people who quietly wanted to strangle me but didn't.

A lot of good came out of The City movement in that it provided Tim Keller, whom I love. I know Timmy K has fallen out of fashion of late with the hardcore Reformed types (EDITOR'S NOTE: This is often what happens when a famous pastor insists on both being reasonable and being orthodox), but I still love the heart and the work, even though I care very little about The City as a thing (note: I still love going to cities).

2010–present: Faux Lumberjack is the pastoral aesthetic wherein you wear dark-wash jeans, Red Wing boots, and a flannel to the pulpit and all of your personal engagements, despite the fact that it's 104 degrees outside because you live in Orlando. Faux Lumberjack pastors smoke cigars and pipes and talk a lot about "masculinity" despite rarely mowing their own lawns, changing their own oil, or ever wielding a saw of any kind.

A lot of good came out of Faux Lumberjack, primarily for the boot and flannel industries, and it was convenient that it coincided with the cigar and beard booms.

2015–present: Wendell Berry wannabes. Wendell Berry wrote very affectionately and very boringly about both the South and the outdoors, which makes him catnip for a certain kind of intellectual pastor or professor, who needs permission to sit outside and read. This is the kind of pastor/professor who constantly threatens to quit his job and become a farmer, despite also being the kind of person who wouldn't last 20 minutes on an actual farm.*

There needs to be a farming fantasy camp for these guys so that for a week every summer, they can get on a tractor and play out their Wendell Berry fantasies. We need to start this company. Farm camp will feature

---

* Excluded from this generalization is my Nebraska buddy Kyle, who loves Wendell Berry, bench presses Buicks, and grew up on an actual farm. He would totally make it as a farmer.

a couple hours a day of actual work, and then about nine hours a day in which pastors can write think pieces in their overpriced leather-bound journals and pontificate about the small amount of fake work they actually did. If we actually started this company and got an A-lister to endorse it, we could all retire in three years.

2019–present: Nothing more can be written about the city, so it's time to write about rural pastors and make it so that the last pastors on earth not to care about persona and book deals can now start being obsessed with those things! The whole *Hillbilly Elegy* memoir craze a few years ago made Christians think that maybe there was something cool about rural areas. **EDITOR'S NOTE:** So did Wendell Berry. Expect a spate of books in this space.

On a somewhat serious note, though, much has been written about the dangers of wanting to be a cool pastor. I think I wrote a chapter in *Why We're Not Emergent* called "Why I Don't Want a Cool Pastor." It still applies to me. Do you guys feel the pressure to want to be cool pastors? I mean, I'm sure we all do/would to some degree. But I feel like now—what with all the political/social posturing happening and the need to kind of always end up on the cool side of those issues to please either people in your congregation (less likely) or people on Twitter (more likely)—it's gotta be a lot of pressure.

RM Now look here, Big T. I have only read one Wendell Berry book, have fewer tattoos than my wife (meaning none), and have a beard too short to be considered a beard by the bearded crowd. Here's the thing about cool kids and pastors who try to look like cool kids: The authentic ones woke up (no pun) one day wearing chucks, flannels, and Levi's without thinking anything about it. Cool is as cool does. But the problem with a conversation about cool pastors is that it invariably turns to pastors who some might label cool but that actual cool kids don't think are cool at all. It's a complicated business, this cool thing, because if you're genuinely cool, you actually see the pastors who don't care about being cool at all as the real cool pastors.

TK I totally agree. Baby, it's like we're selling jeans. Like we're...looking for Fabio.[*]

But seriously, we're so quick to want to distill coolness into an aesthetic or a set of purchases or (more troublingly, I guess) a list of approved authors to like when what's actually cool in a pastor (or, as I think about it, other people) is humility, devotion to the Bible, devotion to the church, and a sense of who they are in light of who God is. So I guess the question is, How do we convince pastors that nobody cares about their boots or their beards or their libraries and that it's the other things that actually matter?

BP The first time I had lunch with Ray Ortlund, an amazing pastor who could not care less about being cool (When he says the word "cool," he is channeling 1960s counterculture 100 percent of the time, and he loves to punctuate a profound sermon point with a Shaggy-from-*Scooby-Doo* style "Like, whoa!" It's awesome and endearing. And not cool.), we met at a yuppie taco joint in Nashville. It was the kind of place that served overpriced, undersized tacos covered in mango salsa on aluminum trays and featuring an impressive/depressing gluten-free selection. (For the record, it was my recommendation, not his.) I got there before Ray, and our waiter, named Rory or Cooper or something, seated me with a "Here you go, bro." Ray walked in a few minutes later bedecked in head-to-toe camo, mud-and-blood-splattered boots, and a grungy ball cap. He had rolled in straight from a deer hunt to meet me. And all I could think was, *I love this man already*.

---

* You'll get this reference if you've watched *Moneyball* at least 50 times, like Big R and I have.

I tell this story to say that (1) nobody has made me see the complete emptiness of cool like Ray and (2) people are drawn to genuineness. You would think that my dad, he of the same tweed-coat-at-every-speaking-engagement, never buy a car manufactured in this decade, and wartime-lifestyle* preaching, might have gotten this message across to me, but it was Ray.

Jesus said, "My sheep hear my voice, and I know them, and they follow me" (John 10:27-28). I think one of the implications of this is that people drawn to Jesus will follow Him whether He is preached by a man with a beard, a man in muddy camo, or a man in a faded tweed jacket. And the people drawn to cool are looking for something else entirely. There is nothing wrong with being fit, dressing nice, and having a modern hairstyle. But if people follow you for *that*, you've got a Carl Lentz's lat-sized problem.

TK I've been to that selfsame aluminum-plate, tiny-taco place with Rory or Cooper. The kind of place where you have to drive by Taco Bell afterward anyway to round out your meal. That place is the Carl Lentz of eating in terms of being all show and no go. And that is an amazing story about Ray and a good word about what we should actually be drawn to.

While we're on the topic of pastoral personas, here are some subspecies of pastoral guys:

The Student: This guy *loves* to study and write papers and is happiest surrounded by volumes of Bavinck and Cornelius Van Til. He's the "the Greek word here *actually* means..." guy when he preaches. He loves to correct the scholarly work of, you know, real scholars (D.A. Carson, Kevin Vanhoozer, Doug Moo, Tom Schreiner, etc.). Early adopter on the "pastors getting

---

* "Wartime lifestyle" is a phrase John Piper coined that refers to eschewing earthly luxuries like the nation did during World War II, only for the sake of Christ's kingdom. It often comes with a side of guilt for having fun or enjoying yourself.

meaningless doctorates" bandwagon. Denominational fits: the OPC (Orthodox Presbyterian Church), the PCA (Presbyterian Church in America), and some strains of the SBC (Southern Baptist Convention; here's looking at you, Midwestern and Southern seminaries). Writing: has several book manuscripts written, but all are severely academic and unreadable. Has been trying to publish his doctoral dissertation for a decade-plus. He'll settle for self-publishing his 14-part sermon series on complementarianism.

The Male Model: This guy spends a lot of money on his wardrobe and is happiest in a coffee shop surrounded by people who can watch him "#working" and making phone calls (from his Bluetooth headphone *or* on speaker phone while he lazily waves his iPhone in front of his face) and is also very happy when posting photographs of himself on Instagram. Loves the hashtag #FitPastor and will absolutely let you know when it's #legday. Does every church announcement video, and, bro, he is *so excited* to announce their upcoming Fit Faith in the Fall series! Loves a wireless handheld mic so he can hold it like a cross between Bob Barker and Ice Cube. Absolute sneakerhead. Denominational fits: any church-planting organization that, name-wise, doesn't sound at all like a denomination. Writing: has an agent and several book ideas in the works but actually has nothing to say.

The Mystic: Happiest when tweeting about his personal Sabbath (but never on his personal Sabbath *or* on his frequent social media sabbaticals), what he has been "recently reflecting on," and social issues or other things that he can make sound ethereal and/or that make him look like a real sweetheart compared to other people. Poses lots of questions with few objective statements, not unlike an undergraduate philosophy student. Denominational fits: would have been emergent in 2004 but is Anglican in 2021. Leans toward Henri Nouwen, Thomas Merton, Richard Rohr, and other touchy/feely "contemplative" guys. Writing: lots of journals.

The Activist: Claims Reformeddom but is happiest when tweeting about how anyone who is complementarian, conservative (politically or socially), white, or male is the worst. Is also definitely white and male. Loves to jump into Twitter conversations between more influential, more famous, more minority people. Strong potential to be an exvangelical by this time next week. Reading habits: Twitter, *White Fragility*, and *New York Times* editorials. Writing: tweets but desperately seeking a coauthor who is a member of any minority group or who is Jimmy Fallon, because Fallon is currently the only straight, white, nonthreatening American male operating (and thriving) in the public eye.

The Douglas Wilson: Happiest when being Douglas Wilson or lighting something on fire (literally or figuratively).

The Congressman: Happiest when laying a biblicalish concept over a political issue and then writing/tweeting/preaching about it at length. Also happy writing long think pieces and has convinced himself that he is a martyr for giving up a sure-to-have-been glamorous career in politics in favor of becoming a pastor. Then again, he didn't really give up politics because he's quietly running a shadow campaign for a denominational president while angling to head up a committee on appointing committee members to oversee committees. Still loves to shake hands and kiss babies. Loves a good power tie. Denominational fits: any. Reading habits: Civil War, World War II, and presidential biographies and any book on anti-wokeness.

The New Yorker: Happiest when talking about "living in New York" while actually being from someplace else, usually a Middle American or mid-Southern regional center sort of city, like Louisville, Memphis, or Omaha. Has lived in New York for six months but has authored or co-authored 16 articles on "living and pastoring in New York City." Strong martyr superiority vibe because he gave up a 2,400-square-foot house to live in a 700-square-foot apartment in Greenpoint. Quietly scoffs at the provincialism of his upbringing as he goes back to delete all online evidence he ever wore a polo and khakis. Reading habits: *First Things, Architectural Digest.* Dabbling in droll humor and having a personality, neither of which is going particularly well.

Somewhat serious question here, though: What happens when a reasonably fashionable person wants to go into pastoral ministry? There's nothing inherently noble about looking like a dork, right? Although there does seem to be something inherently noble/laudable/attractive-in-this-context about a pastor who loves the Word, his flock, and his family more than he loves his own persona. Maybe that's what we're getting at.

RM I think what you're driving at here is self-forgetfulness, baby. It's that sanctified way of being the person God made you but completely at peace with it in such a way that your focus is inherently *others oriented.* At the end of the day, we have to wear *something,* cut our hair like *something,* and choose an image that falls within the parameters of *some* sort of fashion trend. All of this is inescapable. The biggest questions for pastors are, Are your values becoming more shaped by character than clothing? Are you cultivating an image with motivations that seek to satisfy your flesh over your Spirit? Again, it's not really about clothing on your body as much as what's clothing your soul. When we gain freedom from the slavery of image creation, we become free to wear what we want with the same enjoyment that we do anything else that hasn't risen to idol status in our hearts. So wear your Chucks because you like wearing Chucks. Wear your tweed jacket because you like wearing tweed jackets. And while you're at it, set your mind on the things that are above and pray that your passions don't get consumed by consumable things.

Boys, I feel like I just finished writing a sermon but at the kind of length my congregation can only dream of. To summarize, the cool pastor trend has kind of jumped the shark, like all cool trends did a couple of decades ago. When everybody's cool, nobody's cool. When all the cool clothes are available everywhere and everybody buys them and everybody wears them without trying, it means that we're simply material girls living in a material world. Let me repeat what I said earlier: Not caring about being cool is the actual definition of cool. And *that* will never change, no matter how many deep-V, orange-tanned 60-year-old pastors with thousand-dollar sneakers emerge on YouTube.

DOING POLITICAL ENGAGEMENT WELL

TK Here's the calculus: You're white and north of 40, which means the only two ways to really be "okay" culturally* are to be either gay or British. Despite Ron's fetishizing all things British, he's sadly still an American. Sorry, baby, we're all praying for you. Pipe is still white and middle-aged, with the added challenge of being John Piper's son.†

I feel like Ron and Pipe try to be pretty woke‡ despite being middle-aged white guys. For Ron, I think he's taking his cues from Twitter and the crowd he runs with at conferences—meaning theologically sound guys

---

* By this I mean either (a) on white, educated Twitter; (b) in a predominantly white institution of higher learning; (c) on white, educated, Reformed, non-Owen-Strachan Twitter; or (d) in an educated white part of any large to midsized American city.

† Far be it from me to put words in Pipe's mouth. By all accounts (of his), JP was a great dad, and it was great to be his son. I mean more from a "pressure" and "evangelical uncoolness" standpoint.

‡ Let's try to define this word, which is used all the time while being hated by literally everyone: Operatively, I think it means trying to look right as it pertains to all things race/gender/sexuality related.

who want to make painfully sure that people don't confuse them with John MacArthur or the kinds of people who follow John MacArthur or voted for Donald Trump.

For me it's a little less complicated because I'm not a pastor or John Piper's son, but it's still complicated because I work at a university, meaning that wokeness is almost always "in play" as a persona option. I'm not political, I'm not into activism, and I try like crazy *not* to keep up with "the issues," which is impossible in a modern context. That said, I probably spend more time per week with Black guys than anyone I know in that I coach long snappers at a historically Black college (Lane) and coach offensive line for a predominantly Black high school. I love hanging out with Black dudes and have loved it since I was a college athlete and started doing so for the first time. I love their banter and their sense of humor. Nobody busts chops and talks trash like Black dudes. They listen to better music in the locker room. They're a blast. Simply stated, I go where I like it, and I like it there. It's not a good deed, it's not activism, my players are not "projects," and it's not a platforming or leverage thing despite the fact that I just wrote it in a book that will be read almost exclusively by a certain kind of white person.*

That said, I'm probably also not actively making their lives any better, other than (hopefully) treating them very well as their coach and being the best coach I can be, which is a thing I would do for any player of any race. They don't seem terribly interested in seeing me "lament" or even in sussing out the issues, though that does happen from time to time and is always a happy accident. Anyway, I think there's something nice and pure from a friendship standpoint about these guys not having to worry that they're being leveraged by me.

The strange thing, though, is that it all factors into the woke calculus of the 2020s inasmuch as people are always trying to place each other on the

---

* Much like *The Blind Side,* which is a book that I liked but a movie that I hated.

wokeness spectrum and then making inferences and judgments accordingly. For example, because I coach at an HBCU (historically black college and university), people on the campus where I'm a professor (predominantly white) assume that I have an abiding interest in being woke or in wokeness-related issues, which couldn't be further from the truth. Now I *do* have an abiding interest in making sure the Black students and especially Black athletes on our campus feel comfortable and are treated well, but that doesn't mean I want to be invited to or sit through all the "racial reconciliation" meetings that take place on any college campus, are almost exclusively the "productions" of white people, and are meant, at least in part, to make said white people feel more okay about their whiteness.

I know a guy who always has to demonstrate his wokeness by making sure to talk about colonialism and the atrocities perpetrated against Native Americans anytime anybody innocently brings up Thanksgiving, the Cleveland formerly-known-as-Indians-now-known-as-milquetoast-Guardians, or the Washington [redacted]. EDITOR'S NOTE: We are working to confirm whether said guy has already canceled the Atlanta Braves, Florida Seminoles, Utah Utes, American Spirit cigarettes, or the Indian motorcycle brand. He's always down to talk about how small-minded and probably racist our acquaintances are. He is white. When I mention how much I liked Ricky "Wild Thing" Vaughn's haircut in *Major League* (he was a Cleveland Indian), I for sure don't want a lecture on colonialism.

The irony here is that if you're a white guy who tries painfully hard to be woke enough to "say something," people may find you insufferable because nearly all people of all races can tell when something is fake or affected. But as a certain kind of educated white person, you're almost required to affect wokeness from time to time, but it's the requirement that makes me chafe against it more than the issues themselves. Does that make sense?

Further complicating this is the fact that we all have real people in our real (non social-media) lives who we really do care about for whom these issues are way more than just theory. We want to do right by those people. Ultimately, God calls me to love Him and love my neighbor, not to always weigh in on cultural debates and always say the right thing.

There is 100 percent overlap in terms of people I know who describe themselves as "politically engaged" being people who I absolutely *never* want to hang out with. They are, usually, insufferable people. I mean, they may be great people or thoughtful people or very giving/caring people, but they are probably people I don't want to spend a Saturday night with. See also activists. When I was in my MFA (creative nonfiction), it was cool in the poetry track to refer to yourself as an "activist poet," which in most cases was coded language for "a garbage poet." **EDITOR'S NOTE:** They at least had the added bonus of not having to worry about hygiene.

What's hard about the current moment we're in—and in case you're picking up this book in 2035 (if so, God bless you), I'm writing in 2021, which is a sad and disillusioning political hellscape in which every single thing said by every single person is being leveraged by every other person on social media—is that our culture has made it impossible to be politically neutral, because the media has conditioned us to (a) identify an audience and then (b) cater to that audience.

I mean, to me, it all comes down to this: I only have one vote. My wife has one vote. My kids will each have one vote. That's four people in my household whom I could realistically influence one way or another. You can remove my son from that list because he's an Enneagram 8, and therefore you can't tell him anything at all. Tristan, if you're reading this, I love you. You're also for sure not reading this.

What's tough is that we've never gone "political" on the *'Rant* until recently, at which point it made me super uncomfortable because I could almost hear (as we were talking) people unsubscribing for one reason or another. I'm not a pastor, so it would probably be "safest" for me to go polit-ical, except that I hate politics, find it boring, and don't believe in it at all. Ron and Pipe are both trying to walk this fine line of "I want to be woke enough for my Twitter followers and make sure I'm pleasing those people, but not at the expense of alienating the nonwoke people in my congrega-tion." It looks unspeakably hard to me.

How are you boys handling it?

BP Though I didn't realize it at the time, I think I was woke before "woke" meant anything besides the past tense of "wake," at least in the white com-munity. **EDITOR'S NOTE:** "Woke" has a long and illustrious history dating back to the 1930s in the Black community of social, political, and racial aware-ness through changing and uneasy times. Which is to say, I am the hipster of woke. I never saw myself as such until I was accused of being woke (alongside "virtue signaling" and being a "libtard") on Twitter by an account that was a Russian bot, a devotee of Dougie Fresh, or a Southern Baptist pastor; it was hard to tell because the Venn diagram of their respective con-tent is about 86 percent overlap. I always thought of myself as nonpolitical because political parties just looked like denominations minus Jesus plus production value and suits that actually fit. **EDITOR'S NOTE:** While historically accurate, this description fails to note that many denominations are also "minus Jesus," making them even more like political parties. Hooray. And come, Lord Jesus.

In the last few years, though, I've discovered that I am quite political pertaining to issues of justice (abortion, racial inequality, sexuality, etc.). And I have been since I first began to form critical thoughts, postpuberty and pre-drinking age. I grew up in statistically one of the most diverse neighborhoods in the country—a community populated with minori-ties and immigrants from dozens of ethnic backgrounds. My first Little League baseball team was part of a "Cops for Kidz" program trying to keep young punks from becoming criminals. I went to a high school with a large LGBT club before that was cool and before they added the rest of the alphabet. The first person to ever ask me on a date was another guy at that high school. The starting offensive line on my high school football team was composed of two white kids, a Black kid, a Cambodian kid, and an Ojibwe kid. Our left cornerback was a Mexican/Jewish mix, our best wide receiver was Somali, and our QBs rotated between a Black kid with a Greek last name and a kid who was Mexican / Native American.

So I grew up breathing the air of justice issues—or "gospel issues," as white pastors who want to avoid the hard topics call them. I care about these issues personally, societally, and as a pastor. I want my kids to care about them too, despite growing up in a majority-white suburban context. These are moral issues and issues I think God cares about too. I think they matter to the witness of the church. None of which makes me disagree with most of what you said, Ted. Politics, in its current mutant form, has as much to do with issues of justice as Popeyes does with answering the question, Why did the chicken cross the road?

Political engagement sucks. The polarization of it all is soul sucking. And the temptation to try "to be woke enough for my Twitter followers and make sure I'm pleasing those people, but not at the expense of alienating the nonwoke people in my congregation," as you put it, Ted, is enormous. There is no middle ground, and the calls for civility fall on deaf ears. So the temptation to withdraw is as great as the temptation to indulge.

With all that said, my greatest current complaint about politics is that it isn't funny. It can't be funny. It is too bizarre and out of its gourd for jokes. It isn't subtle enough for satire. It's too offensive for laughter. Even our nation's leaders can't be imitated or satirized because they are walking caricatures of leaders already. The last five years of *Saturday Night Live* have proved all this with a bullet. So that leaves us with sincerity, which gets lost in the screaming match, or just participating in the screaming match.

TK Here's what's fun about writing a book with your friends: Pipe, I can honestly say that the above section was some of your best writing, and what's more, I learned a bunch of stuff about you that I didn't exactly know before. That's the joy of reading and writing together. It's like playing basketball with a bunch of buddies and discovering, several games in, that a friend can go to his left (argh, no pun) or has a midrange jump shot. Super fun.

That said, the material above was full of a bunch of interesting takes, and I feel a little convicted that I've withdrawn to a problematic degree. I just don't know how to engage it without being just another strident, leveraging, posturing jerk. But I agree that reclaiming civility seems like a really noble and worthwhile thing to do. I'm compelled to want to try it, but I'm not sure how. And I *really* want to teach my kids to engage with the above issues in a way that moves them (the issues and my kids) forward and doesn't drive them to a posture of being angry and strident. I want them to see and love people like Christ sees and loves them.

Here are a couple of things I struggle with that you two, as men of the cloth, can help me with. One, as an Indiana boy (Midwesterners will feel me on this, I think), I really don't *want* to know where my friends are at politically. It feels like more of a private thing—almost like (stay with me) your sex lives. There are probably a million ways this is unhealthy, but it's a way of saying, "I want to keep connecting with you in all the ways we *do* connect while ignoring the ways we don't connect." For example, the president of the Christian college I went to, who was unabashedly evangelical and an amazing herald of the gospel, was also a Democrat.[*] I knew this about him even back then and then later as I got to know him a little as an adult, but it was *never* the thing he led with or that framed every conversation. I appreciate this about him. I always thought of him as a Christian, a charismatic speaker, a great husband, and a great leader. His politics was way down the ladder in terms of a thing to think about.

Two, I'm not sure how much churches should be addressing this stuff from the pulpit, on either side of the political aisle. For example, my church—which I love with a love that is as childlike and appreciative as it can possibly be for a guy my age—is currently preaching through (depending on who's in the pulpit) 1 Peter and Philippians, and while it (politics) comes up occasionally, it is *never* the focal point. I like this because I'm reminded that it is always about Scripture first and never about using a passage or the pulpit to hammer anyone into a certain perspective politically.

RM Huh.

TK (Sighs) Okay, I'll bite. Care to elaborate a little, baby? This feels a little condescending as is, which I'm sure isn't what you were shooting for. Also, you're really maximizing your payment-per-word here...I think I wanna renegotiate (calls agent, does move[†]). But if we wanna be done talking about politics,[‡] I would be completely fine with that, though this chapter is a little short—even by our standards.

---

[*] As I understand it, more of a labor-union Democrat as opposed to a 2020 Democrat, but still.

[†] This is a long-running in-joke that references the terrible but fun Oliver Stone football movie *Any Given Sunday.*

[‡] Though I would be down for a discussion of political movies, which I—weirdly, like baseball movies—enjoy more than the actual politics themselves. Included in this list are *Frost/Nixon* and *Wag the Dog.*

RM Keep your shirt on, gorgeous, I just need some time to process all the deep thoughts you guys are dishing out. Can a guy get a minute here already?

Look, I've never been one who is drawn much to politics in general. I tend to get overly rational about issues in the sense that I don't believe I have much power to change them just by virtue of holding a particular opinion about them. Now, I'm not saying I don't have opinions about particular issues, because I do, and I can even be passionate about them. But in the past, I've never wanted my passion about an issue that seems too big for one person's opinion to spill over into how I live and breathe. Of course, *that* has changed—or should I say, I've possibly become more sanctified over the years.

I realize that not giving an issue enough thought is a way of giving power to the side of it that may be harmful or damaging to others. In other words, even though I can't personally abolish abortion in America, it matters that I'm passionately and compassionately opposed to it, even if I'm just part of a large collective of voices that believes all of life is sacred. To shrug that off in the name of political ambivalence doesn't seem like a path most glorifying to God, since we need to love what He loves and hate what He hates. And besides that, issues that we like to categorize as "political" are sometimes just a convenient way for us to ignore those who are deeply affected by them in the most damaging and tragic of ways.

As a pastor, this can be like walking a tightrope in that our aim is to herald the gospel, but the gospel has implications that spill over into the realm of the "political" far more often than we're comfortable with, especially if you never want to see your pulpit transformed into a platform for political dance moves. At the same time, sometimes it's unavoidable. When racial tensions hit a fever pitch in the summer of 2020, it would have been irresponsible and cowardly not to mention that men and women of color who are made in the image of God deserve honor, respect, dignity, and equality. The same when it came to the insurrection on the US Capitol. We have to boldly but gently speak out against those who misrepresent the character of Christ, especially when it attempts to broadly paint the church with colors we should never be wearing.

I just read that paragraph and realized how über political I sound right now, which is shocking even to me. But I like the line about political dance moves because it makes me think of Daft Punk holding a reunion show on top of the White House with the president grooving down like he loves the beats while the First Lady reminisces about the time she watched *Saturday Night Fever* with her girlfriends and thought it was SO. CRAZY. I don't know about you boys, but the next time I talk about politics, I'm going to put on a Daft Punk record and see if it doesn't make all the mad people unmad. Because nobody stays mad when there're two French dudes with space helmets turning knobs on analog synthesizers. *Nobody*. **EDITOR'S NOTE:** To Ronnie's great sadness, Daft Punk has since announced that they will be hanging up their space helmets and synthesizers.

TK Huh. Pipe...all yours.

RM Baby, what is Pipe gonna say that you're not gonna say but would like to say if you'd only say it?

TK Keep *your* shirt on, gorgeous. I just think that political "statements" are oftentimes more about the person saying the thing than the people they're supposed to be "helping." And I think we're gonna look back on this weird moment we're in (every pastor talking politics, etc.) as the outlier rather than the norm. But truly, I dialed up Pipe because I think he has more and better things to say than either of us on this. And it's been a while since he's talked.

RM Fine, don't comment on anything I just said. I get how this show works now.

BP Don't worry, boys, my shirt is still on too. Ted, I resonate with what you said (EDITOR'S NOTE: Of course he does) about not wanting to know where other people stand politically. And that used to be how things were, for better or worse. Politics was largely reserved for the voter's booth, and that was as private as a bathroom stall. The old adage was not to discuss politics or religion at the dinner table. Well, to Ronnie's point, those two things are almost inseparable now. Also for better and worse.

On the better side, people are realizing more and more that our Christian convictions must shape our political convictions. If we are to faithfully follow Christ, then we must be advocates and voters for those policies we see as restorative of justice and protective of the weak.

On the worse side, politics and the pulpit are a poisonous mix. We have seen the absolute worst of what happens when the church tries to ride political coattails to power. We have seen "God and country" become "country is God." And we have seen all sorts of mutations and bastardizations of Christianity in the name of political posturing and political parties.

It seems to me that a few things need to define and guide our political engagement.

First, "issues" aren't the issues. People are. People who are image bearers of God and deserve all the dignity, mercy, and respect therein. So when we have strong convictions about an issue, it needs to be on behalf of people and expressed to people, even opponents, with this in mind. If the value of the issue in our mind supersedes the people, we have gotten it backward and are almost sure to fall into idolatry and potentially bigotry.

Second, any political discussion, especially disagreement, is best handled in person. Social media dehumanizes discourse. We begin to feel free to insult and berate others. We misread their words because we have no verbal or physical cues to read. Social media has no tone of voice, no smirks, no earnestness, no humility. So the slightest misunderstanding can derail an entire interaction that could have been fruitful. In person, most of us don't have the stones to insult someone else, and even the most emotionally unintelligent of us can still pick up on body language and tone of voice.

Third, we can disagree and still be friends. It's very un-American, I know, but it's wonderfully Christian. (This will shock some of you, but those two things, American and Christian, aren't actually the same.) "Bear with another." "Love your enemies." These are commands God gave us, and we should follow them. And frankly, if political disagreement leads to actual animosity, you're staking your life on the wrong things. Politics don't define us, Christ does. And in Christ we might come to different political convictions. And that is okay, because no political party has the corner on God. In fact, the three of us disagree on political issues to some degree. You could probably garner some of that through what *isn't* being said in this chapter. But it isn't being said for good reason; friendship matters more than almost any political issue. (Let's hug it out, boys.)

I don't mean to get all teachy. Well, yes I do—I'm authoring. But I feel the tensions you both describe, and they make me want to distance myself from politics and address and engage it too. This is just my best effort at balancing that.

TK Honestly, shouldn't disagreeing and still being friends be the *most* aspirationally "American" thing ever? I mean, isn't this what separates us from a sort of Soviet-gulag mentality in which anyone who dares to step out of line is severely punished until we feel as though they've suffered enough?

The new Twitter orthodoxy would suggest that any rhetorical transgression away from the "theology" of vague-Leftism-meets-influencer-self-help is cause for severe punishment. And even failing to bow and kiss the ring on the regular may be grounds for an online wrist slap. But that said, isn't the coolest thing about America (again, aspirationally) the idea that people from completely different backgrounds and sides of the aisle can come together, accomplish cool things, and even enjoy each other? I mean, Pipe, this is the energy we love about literally every sports movie and war movie ever made.

If we lose that, we lose *Remember the Titans*, *Rocky*, *Friday Night Lights*, *Band of Brothers*, *M*A*S*H*, and all kinds of other things that we say we love.

RM It's all well and good, but we're passionate people, aren't we? Meaning, we like rigorous discourse, and the only thing we like more than that is winning the argument. That's not to discount godly convictions that we feel we need to (at times) defend either. But what you're both getting at is the deal-breaker syndrome, and the evangelical community has become champions of this. Obviously, our positions on certain issues are going to go a long way in establishing how deep our relationship will have the ability to go. For example, I have friends who are Presbyterian pastors, and the fact that they baptize babies in a different tradition than mine has absolutely zero effect on our ability to cultivate deeper friendships. Now, if we ever wanted to be on a church staff together, one of us would probably have to stop baptizing babies, #amirite? The point is that our unity on the most important things outweighs our variances on lesser things.

The church seems to have lost its desire to disagree like Jesus. To be "peaceable, gentle, open to reason, full of mercy and good fruits, impartial and sincere" (James 3:17). What we lack is wisdom from above that moves us in compassion toward one another when conflict rears its ugly head. We've lost the ability to imagine "how good and pleasant it is when brothers dwell in unity!" (Psalm 133:1). To think that a political persuasion, a presidential candidate, or a position on masks and vaccines could divide brothers and sisters who share the broken body and shed blood of Jesus is unthinkable. But it's because the heart of Jesus is not thought about that we end up letting our opinions become Lord and Savior over our lives.

But it doesn't have to be.

DREAM CHASING AND DISAPPOINTMENT

TK So here's why I don't dream: It's Monday, December 21, 2020, which is (of course) four days before Christmas, which will cap—globally and nationally, at least—the worst year we've ever collectively experienced.

I'm standing in my driveway listening to a guy tell me that it'll be thousands to tear up and repair a broken sewer line that is located (of course) under my driveway. I sort of believe him, and what's more, I *have* to, because as a writer and college professor, I am not a plumber and don't really have a clear picture of what's actually happening under my driveway. A day ago, I was ankle-deep in sewage in my crawl space.

Now, I would *love* nothing more than to be the handsome, mysterious, ethereal, dreamer-of-big-dreams guy that I was when my wife married me 24 years ago. **EDITOR'S NOTE:** KK confirmed that Ted was, in fact, handsome, mysterious, and ethereal. That guy had charisma for DAYS and was an absolute blast. **EDITOR'S NOTE:** KK also confirmed this, with a sigh that could only be described as "wistful." Now, however, I am a guy who goes into crawl spaces, fixes flat tires, cleans up puke, cuts the grass, searches for lost cats with a flashlight, repairs broken mowers, unclogs drains, makes runs to the ER when kids need stitches, buys everyone's gifts for Christmas, and occasionally (in my free time) writes and does a day job (professor, journalism). As you can see, in that paradigm, there's very little margin left for dreaming and big-time plan making.

What's interesting about that is that I also, long ago, dreamed of being a husband and a father, which I wouldn't trade but which is the selfsame scenario that makes dreaming a nonstarter, because the more people you bring into your life, the less time you have for thinking/dreaming/planning about your own stuff.

I think in order to really dream-chase at a high level, you have to be either rich or alone, and I am neither. EDITOR'S NOTE: Being alone and functionally poor works too—and adds inspiration.

I think another part of this equation is age. By God's grace, He has allowed me to be a father and a husband. He has also allowed me to write/cowrite/publish 30-plus books, write for magazines, write and make a feature-length film that is eternally in postproduction, play football at a pretty high level in some pretty interesting places (arena leagues, France), live in some completely fascinating and beautiful places (France, Ukraine, Lithuania), and take some pretty killer trips (Israel, all over Europe, the American West, etc.). I have great friends all over the world. I am a member of an absolutely wonderful church where I experience amazing teaching every week. I am *very* thankful for all of this. But part of living these dreams is that you no longer have them as dreams, and you see that, as joyful as they all are, in part, they are still human, broken, and frustrating at times.

What about you guys? Do you dream? If so, what about? And how do you, from a spiritual standpoint, deal with the grinding little disappointments of day-to-day life? I mean, I think I do pretty well spiritually in the "big" moments...but I am admittedly horrible at weathering the grinding and small stuff. I really hate this about myself and am ashamed of my small faith in these times. I confess it—I need Jesus.

BP I've always struggled with dreams—like, I don't know how to do it. I can imagine futures of all sorts of grandiosity and alternate endings. But it feels like writing fiction about my own life. I've never been able to answer the "Where do you see yourself in five years?" question. I'm pretty sure this lost me a couple promotions and job opportunities along the way.

I'm not sure if this is a personality thing or a weird self-protective measure. It protects me from disappointment because I'm never trying to live up to anything I have conjured. Neither, though, am I usually chasing anything, so there's the risk of aimlessness. I especially struggled with this when I was younger. Unlike you, Ted, I don't look back on 24-year-old me jealously (other than about my waistline). I had no real dreams or drive at that point. I just sort of woke up each day and did the job in front of me.

In more recent years, I've realized that rather than dreams of what life should look like, some sort of portrait of success or peace or happiness, I do better by aspiring to be a certain kind of man. Which I guess is a kind of "portrait of success or peace or happiness." So rather than "I want to accomplish such-and-such someday," which feels like a road to pride or disappointment, or "I want to have a life like so-and-so someday," which could lead to jealousy and disappointment, I try to think, "I want to have the character of so-and-so" or "I want to love my wife like so-and-so." It helps set a trajectory for me, and it works as a sort of measuring stick. I certainly don't live all the way up to those aspirations, but it feels like there is room for growth, and I can see how far I have come.

RM This is a massive thing for me, so I resonate with Big T quite a bit. **EDITOR'S NOTE:** Of course you do, Enneagram 4. Dreaming about the future is part and parcel of who I am. To a fault. Like a San Andreas–level fault. Dreaming composed so much of my growing up that it's been an incredibly difficult area to find some spiritual maturity and sanctification in. To begin with, dreaming has always been attached to hope. It is this idea of "what may be" that has driven so many of my pursuits, so it's true that when something is actually achieved, however big or small, there's an inevitable letdown because it ceases to be something to dream about and hope for any longer.

TK Baby, you're literally speaking my language. I've been living that life for decades. It was just always so easy to throw another book or another project into the gaping maw of my heart. That said, that stuff no longer works anymore (more on that below), so I think I may be closer to where God wants me on this matter.

RM I think age begins to introduce disillusion, which is no bad thing, because we don't want any parts of our lives to be illusory, do we? It's not that we don't understand that these things don't satisfy us at some micro-level; it's that we are so enraptured by the microtonal quality of a lesser dream coming true. This obviously gets us to the "mud pies" illustration that Clive Lewis so aptly laid out for us, but I think we tend to like mud pies quite a bit. A mud pie is easy to make, the ingredients are right at your fingertips, and you can keep making those things to your heart's content. A mud pie bakery, man. Everyone has one in their backyard ready to start building an inventory with. Like, I'm already excited just thinking about how easy it'll be to start a venture like this.

Except nobody wants to eat them. It's an infantile fantasy. It's an exercise in adolescent playacting. And that's an illustration of what our dreams have the potential of becoming when they're composed of less than spiritually edible qualities.

TK I always thought the mud pie thing was Pipe's dad.

RM Seashells, baby. Seashells. But I think spiritual maturity is the realization that, first off, dreams come from the Lord. He's given some of us the mind to dream creatively and lavishly along with the sense of wonder to imagine what might be if certain things come to fruition. If we embrace this truth of how God created us to be, we will be prone not to give up our dreams but to give our dreams over to the One who can fulfill them in a way where hope increases instead of diminishes after expectations have been met but really unmet because of the flatness it produces inside. I'm not sure of anything I struggle with more than this, boys. I like my mud pies.

TK Speaking of, I'm currently three years into writing and coproducing a feature film called *Silverdome*, which I rarely regret doing, save for the fact that it may be killing my dream of being a filmmaker inasmuch as dreaming about something is almost always way better than actually doing it. I wrote this, about the process, a couple of years ago:

> My producer called the night before our production company was to begin shooting at the old Pontiac Silverdome in Detroit. "Both actors are in tears," he explained. "And people are being thrown out of hotel rooms." The line went silent for a moment as I tried to think of how to respond. "The good news is, this is happening now and not in the middle of the shoot," he said, ever the optimist.
>
> I wrote a script a couple of years ago about a fictional ex-USFL quarterback who leaves his home, job, and family in the midst of an existential crisis to live as a squatter in the abandoned Pontiac Silverdome. The Silverdome was once the world's premiere domed venue. It was home to the NFL's Detroit Lions and the

NBA's Detroit Pistons as well as Super Bowl XVI, Wrestlemania 3, and many other sports and popular culture milestones.

I almost sold the script to an actor whose name you would recognize, who wanted to turn it into a concussion story—that is, to make the main character punchy and pitiable. I didn't want to go that route, so I hung on to it...figuring it was the end of my project. However, a year or so ago, shortly after moving to Jackson, I showed the script to Glenn Pakulak, a former All-SEC and NFL punter and current actor, and he fell in love with the story and the character.

"I felt like you told the story of my life and of so many former players," he said after reading it. "We have to make this." Glenn enlisted the help (read: funding) of several former NFL buddies, and soon we were forming an LLC, finding a producer and director, and setting about the herculean task of making a feature-length low-budget independent film.

Today I'm reclining in a trailer, on the set of my own movie. It's surreal. Also in the trailer is Carmen Serano, best known for her work on AMC's critically acclaimed show *Breaking Bad*, and an unspeakably handsome young actor named Cisco Posada, who has a recurring role on Fox's record-industry drama, *Empire*. We're all marveling over the '90s tech in the trailer, the most remarkable feature of which seems to be the sofa that mechanically slides back about six inches, thereby, theoretically, "opening up" the living room of the trailer. Cisco is especially thrilled by this. "That is so dope," he says.

Chris Regner, our producer, is poring over budgets and looking for ways to conserve cash, as is the lot in life of the indie producer. He lived in Hollywood for several years trying to write when, as it turns out, he was an incredibly gifted producer all along. I've known Chris for 15 years—to see him excel in this role is a thrill.

In the back of the trailer, Thani Magnusson, a 2016 Union University grad, runs lines with Elizabel Riggs, another Union alum. They are former students, and it's a thrill to know them in this context—grown-up and professional.

In a few minutes, I'll go outside with my friends, and we'll film a scene that I wrote, except that instead of little kids sword fighting in my folks' backyard and filming it on an '80s camcorder, we'll do it for real this time.

That is so dope.

It was equal parts a super fun experience and also a thing that occasionally wakes me up with night sweats and terror that we'll never get it done and never pay our investors back. Still, it was the fulfillment of a dream.

Our culture has an interesting relationship with dreams. I think in secular America, your dreams are all you have—whether it's dreaming about a business conquest, a trip, or some other accomplishment. From a young age, we're told to follow our dreams, which implies having dreams. This was never hard for me as a kid. In fact, I used to sit in a rocking chair every day after school, turn on music, and just dream. I would dream about where I wanted to live, the girl I had a crush on, football, and achievements. I would dream of being a more confident and accomplished person than I was currently. It's weird—I now don't trust middle-aged guys with big dreams.

BP This is all fascinating to me because I don't understand it at all. You've both written so clearly and painted such a vivid picture...of something that is as real to me as Narnia or Hogwarts. Maybe it's because I was never told to follow my dreams. My entire upbringing was in the context of "God is sovereign" and "Seek the Lord's will for your life." Combine that with a general sense of do-what-seems-best-and-move-on-to-the-next-thing, and

I don't recall ever having had dreams for my life. My nature blended really well with a nurture that was suspicious of dreams. I wasn't inclined toward them, and my theological atmosphere suppressed them. (Also, watching overly energetic entrepreneurial or artistic friends fail to take flight was, um, disenchanting.)

I have definitely experienced disappointment, but it almost always lands on me later (excluding those times of outright pain, betrayal, etc.). It's as if I didn't know what I hoped for or expected out of something until that something fails to deliver. *Then* I realize I wanted more from it. It's usually a low-grade fog of disappointment rather than a piercing or crushing thing.

For better or worse, I live my life more in terms of "What is the next right thing?" and "What trajectory does this put me on?" rather than dreams and detailed pictures of a fully formed future. I focus most on the things I see as in my control. Am I using my gifts well? Am I developing a Christlike character? Am I growing as a husband and a dad? My perspective is that if I handle these things, invest in them, and give them my attention, the future takes care of itself.

This means I spend a lot more time and energy and reflection looking back at where God has brought me than looking ahead at where I want to go. I can dream for our church. I can dream with other people. But when it comes to my own life, I focus almost entirely on right now and on where I was—more trajectory than destination.

(RM) Well, golly, Pipe, looks like you have this all figured out and need to write a book called *Dreams? What Dreams?* But in all seriousness, "dream avoidance" is a way to protect yourself from disappointment, but I would argue that even that is still a dream in and of itself. The avoidance of a dream is just another way of hoping for a different outcome in some category of life. If we distill dreams down into "the hope of something better in the future," then all of us are dreaming all the time because we're unable to do anything else. Even asking one of the questions Pipe asked like "Am I growing as a husband and dad?" is aspirational and dreamlike in nature.

As people, we are living on either the threads or the ropes of hope at all times. Even when hope is like a thread, we're still holding on to it like a rope. Even when we say we have no hope, we can't help but desire an outcome that will somehow materialize in the vacuum we imagine ourselves to be in. Dreams are really the fruit of imagination in some ways. To say "I wish" or "I wonder" is to imagine a world that is more desirable and ideal than the one you're currently in. And we are all wishers.

BP Ronnie, I'm not sure that it's fair (EDITOR'S NOTE: We all knew this would bother Pipe) to call what I do "dream avoidance" any more than it would be fair to call what I do on a daily basis "flying avoidance." When you and T describe how you dream and think, I don't cringe or duck or feel anxious. I just try to imagine what it must be like to go through life with such clear pictures of how you'd like the future to be or experiences to come to fruition. It doesn't scare me any more than the thought of flying with wings I don't have.

I *do* think dream avoidance is a way to avoid pain. No expectations = no disappointment, right? Sort of, but it also means never experiencing the pleasure of "It's *all* happening!" I think dreamers who have been crushed can easily pendulum-swing this way as a self-protective measure. EDITOR'S NOTE: Barnabas wrote about this in his book *Hoping for Happiness*.

But I don't think that's me. My mind and heart just work differently. I remember releasing my first book and being totally stumped when people asked, "What are you hoping for out of this?" I did the work to write the best thing I could at the time. I hoped it would help folks. But I didn't have big dreams or expectations for it; it was just the next right thing for me to do with my gifts and time. So when it didn't hit the *New York Times* bestseller list (or any other list for that matter, thank you very much TGC), I wasn't crushed. When it wasn't selected for any of the 722,312 end-of-year booklists, I wasn't crushed. And neither was I swept away by the bliss of "birthing my book baby." **EDITOR'S NOTE:** "Book baby" is what many Internet influencers call their book releases, and it's no less crazy than being a "dog mom." Both cases require a weird sort of interspecies breeding and an odd gestation. I don't think I ever shed a tear or lost a wink of sleep (over that book or any other that I've written) out of disappointment or delirium.

I think I experience the "It's all coming together" pleasure in the same way I experience disappointment—after the fact, as a dawning realization. It means I have to conscientiously reflect on the good so I don't miss the ways God blessed. And I have to conscientiously reflect on the bad so I don't just charge past pain like it never happened.

So here's a question for you: Does it seem to born dreamers, like the two of you, that people like me are emotionally stunted or defective, because from Ronnie's previous comments, it kind of seems like it?

TK That's a great question, and I'm gonna answer it momentarily, after I address the "book baby" thing: There are few instances in which I could actually envision killing...but the "book baby" thing fills me with white-hot rage. But I think the rage speaks to this at some level. One, the "book baby" thing is just inane and stupid and cloying* and needy, and I hate it. Two—and more apropos of this discussion—there's something in me that is *jealous* of the stupid, inane influencer's excitement (or even faux excitement) vis-à-vis their undoubtedly insipid and forgettable† new book.

---

* Look at me! Look at my book! Look what I achieved! (Couched in a so-thin-as-to-barely-be-there veneer of humility.)

† See, here's the thing: All children are God's handiwork—beautifully and wonderfully made in His image. Most books—especially by "influencers"—are stupid and forgettable.

Meaning, there's a part of me that actually *wants* to feel that way about my own projects. But I don't. I feel a vague sense of satisfaction that the project is finished, and I occasionally feel proud of the project itself. But I never feel like I've just brought the literary equivalent of a child into the world. I think publishing a whole bunch of books has given me a pretty low view of the whole thing, to be honest. Not in a cynical way, but just in a "a thing is gradations less exciting/cool/memorable after you've done it several times" way.

To your question, Pipe (and it's a good one): I'm actually jealous of you too. I wish I could go into situations or even the vague, amorphous "future" with little to no expectation for any of it. I wish I could have the "even keel" experience of not being too let down by anything. I think people with your makeup generally lead happier, healthier lives on the whole. Your highs aren't too high, and your lows aren't too low. I would love to be a little more emotionally stunted.

I mean, here's what I've done today: cut the grass, worked out, cleaned out the inside of my wife's van, bought something for my kid online. I'm doing a little writing (on this). I haven't planned a vacation, sold a screenplay, had any headshots taken, or done anything remotely glamorous or celebrity oriented. This is life. This is the norm. We live in a world that is decaying, and our bodies, homes, vehicles, and even capacity for dreaming all bear that out.

So to summarize: I'm jealous of both the delusional, ridiculous, middle-aged, slimeball, leadership dreamers and the nondreamers alike. But I respect the nondreamers more.

That said, I think the Lord has brought me some distance on this matter in that I no longer look too far into the future and no longer have huge expectations for specific projects or my career in general, and I'm finding it easier to be a little more content in the day to day. I'm finding myself as delighted by (or perhaps even *more* delighted by) a quiet evening with KK than a new contract or a new product release or even the presence of some big dream in my life. I want to cultivate this, and I pray that the Lord would give me more of it.

RM I think age and maturity have given me, a man prone to wandering into the world (wasteland?) of dreams and fantasies, some measure of sobriety. **EDITOR'S NOTE:** Dream avoidance might help too. But dreams have always been tied to hope for me. I grew up in a rural community where I lived an hour from school, didn't have a lot of neighbors (read: friends), and spent the majority of my time playing...and dreaming...alone. In some ways, I don't know if I was born a dreamer or if it came packaged as part of the culture I was thrust into at eight years old. Whatever it was, dreaming was how I learned to hope. *Someday I hope to be this person, Someday I hope to accomplish this thing, Someday I hope my life looks like this.* It all turned out to be a misshapen hope because I was at the center of it all, building expectations that would inevitably not be met and would need to be reckoned with spiritually. That reckoning is still happening, by the way.

Of course, by God's grace, our dreams can become redeemed. Those adolescent aspirations of mine that came cloaked in youthful arrogance have either vanished completely or become far more redemptive in nature.

Reflecting on all this today, the story of Jacob comes to mind. I think about him obtaining his brother's birthright, getting the wife he desired from his uncle, and acquiring an insane amount of material wealth through years of hustle and bustle. And just like that, the chase was over, and Jacob had to square up with God and a brother who had threatened to kill him the last time they chatted. Jacob's dreams needed to be redeemed, and his wrestle with God—and the limp that ensued—allowed him to see that peace with God is better than the realization of personal dreams.

Whether we identify as lofty dreamers or level-headed pragmatists, we still carry hopes that need to be redefined and redeemed because they will demand our worship otherwise. To hold a dream before the Lord is an exercise in humility because we're saying that His design for our life is worthier than our desire for the life of our dreams. To see Jacob bow before his brother in humility was the actual dream God had been preparing Jacob for during all his years of scheming and conniving. It's the place God has for all of us as the One who doesn't remove our dreams but reshapes them into the dreams they were always meant to be.

THE CHRISTIAN ADDICTION TO PERSONALITY TESTS

TK The Enneagram is amazing because it couches our natural narcissism in a thin veneer of both "spirituality" and academic introspection. When what you're really doing is just spending a whole lot of time thinking about yourself.

I actually kind of enjoy Enneagram stuff, were it not for the fact that I absolutely cannot stand other 4s (I'm a 4w3). **EDITOR'S NOTE:** A 4w3 is a four wing…never mind. Literally everyone reading this book knows this, which speaks to the Enneagram's cultural takeover. When I hear them talk, there's almost a 100 percent chance that I want to punch them in the throat. Which raises the question, Do I sound like that? Probably. Do I hate myself? Probably.

There is no chance that I can listen to any Enneagram podcast, much to the chagrin of my wife, who really wishes I could listen to them and discuss them.

It's hard because being my age (I'm Gen X), I naturally identify with the '90s, which was the decade of being disdainful of literally everything. So my impulse is to make fun of the Enneagram and Myers–Briggs, except that I (guilty pleasure) really enjoy both of them and can talk about them almost indefinitely.

Because I did my first handful of Christian books with Moody Publishing, I probably owe my Christian writing career to Gary Chapman inasmuch as the *Five Love Languages* stuff was basically a Brink's truck that would just back up to Moody Publishing every year and dump cash on them, allowing them to finance all of their other (ahem) tepidly selling books, many of which were mine. Shout-out to Gary Chapman.

Semiserious question: If we think of all the other evangelical trends we've lived through as being in a giant trash heap, is the Enneagram going to end up there soon? And if so, where will it end up?

BP I worked at Moody Publishers for a couple years in the mid-2000s and can confirm this description is 100 percent accurate. I can also confirm that Gary Chapman is wonderful (what those in Hollywood might call a "lovely man"). He is humble and gracious and unassuming and all the things we wish superfamous people would be.

That said, I prefer to think of these past trends as an "archive" rather than a trash heap. That way we can take them back out to revise and reintroduce them periodically. Or just make jokes at their expense.

I would bet good money that every reader of this book can name their love languages, even if they have never heard of Gary Chapman. (Which means, dear reader, you missed the point. You're supposed to be able to name the love language of your significant other or else this whole thing falls apart.) Somehow what was a "Christian" trend became cultural currency. I think the Enneagram has gone this route and is not going anywhere. Once you get to the point where people make their entire living by "certifying" themselves as "coaches" and doing workshops for entire churches and

companies, that thing isn't going away real quick. **EDITOR'S NOT**
tifications have about as much veracity and authority as the c
gets at the end of a cookie-decorating class at the local comm
We haven't even scratched the surface of the potential of (read: m
be made off) the Enneagram. There are more books, more podcasts, more
webinars, more conferences, more calendars, more newsletters, and more
counseling curricula to come. Which of course means there is a whole *other*
cottage industry to be built around WHY THE ENNEAGRAM IS EVIL,
because that's what Christians do.

I'm just not sure which route to go. Should I certify myself as an Enneagram coach or should I start a YouTube channel about how heinous it is?

🆃🅺 Well, I'm sure I'm not alone in expressing that I would just love to see
a Piper YouTube channel of any kind. That said, can I express something
here in writing that's been bothering me for a long time? Unless you're preparing a team of some kind (sports, debate, whatever) for competition,
you're NOT a coach. I push back on the idea—on behalf of all real coaches
everywhere—that a guy named Trevor in a quarter zip, with a scented candle in his office, asking you whether you feel more like a 7 or an 8 is a
"coach."

I've made my peace with the fact that Enneagram "coaches" exist, but
can we just call them something different? **EDITOR'S NOTE:** Some titles to
consider instead of coach would be "master," "swami," "sensei," "guide,"
"sherpa," or "con artist." Also, and hear me out on this, Enneagram feels
like a fine thing to talk/think about around the dinner table (or whatever)
but a really dumb thing to spend any amount of money on. I feel like if I'd
sprung for a conference or a "coaching" session, I would immediately feel
like, "Yep, took it too far. This is dumb."

Here's a thing that happened recently re: Enneagram: Kristin and I
watched a 2019 version of *Little Women* that was amazing, and by the third

nneagram-typed all the sisters and the mom[*] and the old guy
xt door and the kid with the girl's name (Laurie[†]) who should
the girl with the guy's name (Jo[‡]). It (the Enneagram typing)
experience but one that in the cold, harsh light of day I am
t.[§] Should I be?

at I feel like within the Enneagram-is-god cir-
one is starting to experience Enneagram fatigue.
And   at is, we're growing tired of every conversation ending with.   ite "That's so 8 of you" or "How *very* 9 of you to say that"
or "Spoke   e a 2!" What you come to realize with the Enneagram, like
any personality-based test (so help me if you come at me with the whole
"Enneagram is not a personality test" argument), is that humans are far too
complex to be categorized with such neatness. I'm not saying it can't be
helpful; I'm saying that it's only helpful to a point.

More than fading out, I think it might be that it's losing its luster for
some of the early adopters. The problem is that no matter how much
you learn about yourself or others with the Enneagram, you're still forced
to face who you are, which is always going to be a problem. Obviously,
self-knowledge is good, because it goes hand in hand with knowledge of
God, but the human condition doesn't end because we've all discovered our

---

* Probably a 2.

† A 7 or 4.

‡ An 8 or a 3.

§ We've done the same thing with all the *Downton Abbey* characters too. If you want to
hear Ron and me go into great detail on this in our spinoff pod *Happy Abbey*, drop us a
note at info@happyrantpod.com.

Enneagram numbers and we can have funny and fabulous conversations about it with pseudointellectual friends at dinner parties.

It also carries the potential danger of "Sorry, I'm a 6. This is just who I am, so deal!" Translated: Don't expect me to behave, change, or transform into a more sanctified person that you'd actually want to be at a dinner party with.

I've said dinner party twice now, which is sooo 4 of me.

🇹🇰 Good stuff here, baby. I'm "pro" dinner party. I think the problem with this Enneagram stuff, for us, is that it's hard to leverage it as a 4 because our thing is almost universally unlikable. People would never accept "Sorry, I'm just a 4, and being self-absorbed and maudlin is just who I am, so deal!" Come to think of it, the same thing is probably true of Pipe's 8 stuff.

Speaking of dinner parties...what's your ideal dinner party, Enneagram-wise*? I'm thinking I need a 7 at the table to laugh at all my jokes, an 8 at the table to have some decent convictions about things, a 3 to talk about their work stuff incessantly and give us all somebody to roll our collective eyes at, a 5 to tell me what to do about my stock portfolio, and a 9 to insist that everybody else eat first and that it doesn't matter what we eat because they are good with anything.

🇷🇲 That's a spectac dinner party arrangement, baby. Except by the end of the night, a 7 will exhaust you, an 8 will be tired and grumpy, a 3 will just be telling lies, and a 5 will attempt to divert every casual convo into something more "real." Oh, and if you invite any 6s, I'll have to politely decline the invite.

Other than that, great party, T.

---

* Do I hate myself for asking this? I do.

TK Fascinating, baby. Where you at with 6s? Bad experience?

RM Umm. You could say that, yeah. (Not all 6s, to be clear.)

BP The very thought of a "dinner party" leaves me tired and grumpy. (That's so 8 of me.) They always sound to me like one big fun-measuring contest. Who is the funniest? (7 or 8w7.) Who has the keenest insights? (5, but he doesn't know when to stop.) Who is the nicest? (9.) Who tells the best stories? (7 or 3, if people don't know him well enough to know he's spewing BS.) Who got a promotion? (3.) Who did we vaguely enjoy but forget was there because they spent most of the time asking, "Does anyone need anything else?" even if it's not their house? (2.)

Even before the Enneagram, dinner parties felt to me like a competition where all the couples leave and talk crap about each other on the way home or yell at one another because "I can't believe you *said* that!" (Also, so 8 of me.) The numbers just make clearer who I am annoyed at and about what.

(I feel the need to add that I love having dinner with friends—whole groups of friends—and yet-to-be friends. I like meeting people and getting to know them. I like laughing with people and listening to people tell their stories. None of this, however, sounds like a "dinner party." And none of this has any numbers involved, except maybe pouring a second round, and none of it is a contest.)

All of this leaves me wondering, Is there a good version of personality tests? Or maybe a better way to ask this is, Is there a version of personality tests that we won't use to reduce other people to a number (or a love language, or four letters, or five strengths, or whatever)? And is there a version that won't walk us into the trap of personal petrification where "I'm an 8, and this is just who I am"?

RM I think you're describing our tendency to judge others and having the perfect outlet to do it. On one hand, a personality test allows us to see who we are and to potentially self-deprecate through the weaknesses that it sur-faces. Much more enticing is to look at others' tests and become far less, umm, generous. It's probably fun to point out that Paul didn't seem to bring up Timothy's Enneagram or Myers–Briggs scores to help this dude become a better pastor. **EDITOR'S NOTE:** Paul may have kicked John Mark to the curb because he was an Enneagram 6. **EDITOR'S SECOND NOTE:** And that would be totally justifiable. Paul may have been an Enneagram 8, but he describes himself as "wretched" before encouraging Timothy to be a less timid leader. I think the word for the day when it comes to personality tests is "humility," because believing that they create a straight path into the innermost complexities of the soul is treating them a little too much like witchcraft. Which, if you like essential oils and personality tests, is right up your occultic alley. Boys, I've been lying awake at night trying to think of a way to bring essential oils and witchcraft into the convo, so now I can sleep.

TK Baby, you just alienated my wife and all her friends by taking shots at essential oils and personality tests. Those two things are the diffused air they breathe. I'm going to end up paying for that comment. **EDITOR'S NOTE:** Not as much as she already paid for essential oils.

RM Cool, cool.

BP First of all, the apostle Paul was most definitely a 1. SO precise. SO self-flagellating (chief of sinners and whatnot). **EDITOR'S NOTE:** Only an Ennea-gram 8 would tell you he's sure of what Enneagram the apostle Paul was.

But to Ted's question about "good" versions of personality tests, I think the answer is no. Which is to say, I don't think there is a version of a personality test that won't make us selfish and self-centered in about six minutes. We made the *Five Love Languages* into "how to love me" instead of using it to understand others. We turned the Meyers–Briggs into an excuse to avoid certain people or work environments. We turned StrengthsFinder into an excuse to focus only where we naturally excel and ignore the areas we suck. And we've used the Enneagram as an opportunity to understand ourselves more and more and more deeply rather than understanding others. (Which, of course, means we are actually gaining a less accurate understanding of ourselves.)

Somehow all this self-love, self-study, and self-understanding doesn't resemble healthy self-awareness. You know, the kind that recognizes my place in society and my inherent value as a human as well as everyone else's and leads to actual empathy. ("Empathy" has somehow become a byword in certain Reformed theological circles. Probably because "feelings" are terrifying for some people. Or because an attempt to actually grow in empathy would be really difficult and require actually listening to and caring about others. All "empathy" means is "the ability to understand and share the feelings of another." That is a good thing. It's the entryway to compassion, a trait Jesus was known for.) We've gotten no better at understanding ourselves through these tests, and we might have actually gotten worse.

Buckle up for classic preacher whiplash here: I think that's because no personality test accounts for sin. Ronnie mentioned humility and pride earlier, and that was spot-on. Those are fruits of the human heart, either of the Spirit or of the flesh. Personality tests deal in vague morality and usually try to be morally neutral. But the human heart is never morally neutral. So a test that seeks to categorize people without acknowledging the single most powerful driving force in our lives is going to fail.

The question this raises for me is, Does this mean we should pitch all personality tests, or is there a way to use them that actually takes sin into account?

RM First off, good question, Pipe. Secondly, a cursory reading of Romans 1 and the entire book of Galatians puts Paul squarely in the Enneagram 8 category. And I would guess that he had a high percentage of Enneagram 1 too. **EDITOR'S NOTE:** If Paul was an 8, he was a very "resourceful" 8.

It'll be my first question to Paul when I get to heaven: "Hey, Paul, big fan here. Just wanted to say good work on Romans 8, by the way. Curious, before we head over to the feast: What's your Enneagram number? I'd love to know..."

To your question, Pipe, I think some of the more redemptive Enneagram sessions I've sat through have taken sin into account fairly well, which is why they use the categorization of "unresourceful" (sinful) to describe certain behaviors that correspond with specific types. Only someone versed in the gospel is going to define "unresourceful" this way, of course. But I think to ditch personality tests would be a mistake. I say let's receive them humbly, acknowledge their limitations, and be willing to reshape them so that we allow Scripture to give us an even more accurate readout.

But your point about sin is...umm...on point. But how much of this is nature versus nurture?

TK That's a good question, baby. Here's how I look at it: If I take my 4w3-ness and choose to say about the 3 part, "Look, I'm just a shame-driven, achievement-driven, self-centered jerk of the highest order, and, per the Enneagram, that's JUST WHO I AM!" then some of that is "nature" (i.e., I was born with it), but I'm choosing to nurture it. Similarly with the maudlin, mopey, equally self-centered 4 stuff. I think the Enneagram may be giving lots of people permission to be the worst versions of themselves. Nowhere is the Bible really ever saying, "You're okay to indulge and even nurture your most sinful attributes/impulses because that's just how you are."

To your "nurture" question: Maybe I'm a 3w because my dad never said "Good job,"* and maybe I'm a 4 because I never auditioned for a high school

---

* Pops, if you've read this far—and I kind of hope you haven't—you absolutely said "Good job." This is just an example.

play, and that was my deepest secret longing.* I'm being glib, but you get what I mean. To that I say, to some degree, who cares? Figuring out why I'm the way I am seems, these days, to take a rather large backseat to (Lord willing) fixing it before it's too late. Maybe that's a function of age.

Even a word like "unresourceful" carries with it an insane amount of glossing over as it pertains to the sin issue. We would never say, "Hey, I slipped into a moment of unresourcefulness when I cheated on my wife" or "It was really unresourceful of me to completely aggrandize myself while cutting someone else down just then." It looks ridiculous to us in part because *it is ridiculous*. If a thing isn't encouraging me to look at my sins for what they are and then repent of them, I question the veracity of that thing (see also much of pop psychology).

To Pipe's question, I think we *could* pitch them and lose almost nothing. In a couple of weeks, we'd barely notice they were gone because there's still plenty of Bible to study, there are plenty of good commentaries to read, and there are plenty of real people in our lives who need our attention. But to Ron's good point, I don't think we have to. As with most things in our lives, there's a moderation window we're endeavoring to fall into.

Here's where I think things like the Enneagram really succeed: as entertainment. After we've watched all the Netflix and Amazon Prime shows and tweeted all the things about them (which are actually about ourselves), the Enny still gives us an almost academic context in which to talk about ourselves, which is the most entertaining thing there is. I mean, that's the implicit promise in every Enneagram podcast pulling listeners right now: "Listen to this thing that is basically about you."

It's hard to walk away from it.

---

* There's actually some truth to this.

EVANGELICAL MONEY GUILT

TK From age 0 to age 18, I was blissfully unaware of money. I grew up in a blue-collar industrial and agricultural town where, by and large, nobody had much money. I mean, there were those kids in school who had new Jordans and nice jeans, but for the most part, if you were lucky enough to have a car, you were driving a hand-me-down from a dad or an older sibling.

Then I went to Taylor University, which is an upscale Christian college nestled right in the middle of nowhere, about 15 minutes from where I grew up. That's where I was introduced to the idea that there were lots of wealthy kids* driving Lexuses to college and walking around the dorm in supernice North Face jackets while planning their future ski trips. I was like the Chris O'Donnell character in *Scent of a Woman* in terms of not having any money or ski trips. Again, for 18 years, this didn't bother me.

At Taylor, everybody came from money in some form or fashion,

---

* A recent text from my friend Cory while watching a Steelers game: "Roethlisberger to Freiermuth sounds like two dorms at Taylor." He won the evening with that one!

including the girls that I might potentially date. I had developed such a complex about it that on my second date with the woman I ended up marrying, I had developed a speech that I laid on her as I drove her in my parents' Buick Century* to our dinner date in Indianapolis. I probably delivered the speech somewhere around Anderson, and it went something like this:

Me: "I really, really like you, but I just want you to know right now, up front, that I don't come from money, I don't have lots of money, and I may never have lots of money."

Kristin, my wife of 24 years and counting: "That's ridiculous, and you are ridiculous. Who do you think I am?"

We then, probably, made out, inasmuch as we dated and married before *I Kissed Dating Goodbye* became a thing. EDITOR'S NOTE: Not to disparage Ted, and definitely not to disparage KK, but this was also well before True Love Waits. Otherwise, there would have been absolutely no making out. Anyway, with the money speech out of the way, we embarked on a fast and furious romance that culminated in a summer invitation to Kristin's family's "cottage" on an idyllic spring-fed lake in Northern Michigan. When I heard "cottage," I thought of "tiny log cabin" because I had never been to a cottage in the sense of "a place that rich people go to in Northern Michigan." She informed me, gently, that the cottage was more of a house, and a huge one.

Because it was the '90s and I was intimidated, I did what any good '90s weight-lifting meathead would have done and utilized my friend Russell's mom, who worked at a video store in town that doubled as a tanning parlor. She allowed me to do all of the free tanning I wanted to do, which as a pale, Germanic type, wasn't much, but I at least arrived at Torch Lake with a nice, golden-brown tan to go with some great, floppy, '90s hair. Shout-out to Mrs. Russell.

---

* Which I detailed by hand, earlier that day, as a means of making the date "perfect."

The cottage looked like it came from a magazine and featured a framed set of "house rules," which were taken very seriously by everyone involved, which turned out to be Kristin's parents, grandparents, brothers, and the brothers' love interests at the time. If there was a term for "panic attack" in the '90s, I probably had several on that trip. The trip involved me, a college athlete, sucking at a ton of "sports" that blue-collar Midwestern kids don't play, which includes but is not limited to waterskiing, ultimate Frisbee, Frisbee golf, and a card game called Dutch Blitz, which was dizzying and a lot to deal with. I longed for a cruddy weight room, and I think I even found one in town, which I went to for a little "mental health time."

The low point of the trip was some campfire time, which included her rich uncle (who stayed in the "cottage" next door) asking me, "Where do you see yourself in five years?" At which point I shrank a few feet and then died. He definitely "won" that interaction, which is a thing that matters to a lot of guys who end up becoming rich uncles. EDITOR'S NOTE: Rich uncles are usually Enneagram 3s or 8s.

Thankfully, I was in love and would have gone into vast amounts of debt to secure Kristin's hand in marriage.

The money thing is a weird one because while evangelicals have a well-founded reputation for being unspeakably cheap and trying to get everything for free, Reformed guys I've met fall into two categories. This first category is the cheap guys—pretty standard. The second, though, is the Reformed guy who is so hypercapitalist that he thinks his way of "making a point" in a culture gone Marxist is to channel his inner Gordon Gekko and go all 1980s conspicuous consumption. [Redacted] has baptized this guy's greed in a thin veneer of spirituality. EDITOR'S NOTE: For fear of being sued, we will simply say this guy's name rhymes with Rave Mamsey.

These guys are fun to hang out with because they always have the best of everything and, as a result, eat and relax at a really high level. They can get a little insufferable though, because as soon as a guy gets a little money in his pocket, he immediately becomes an authority on literally everything from the government to how your favorite baseball team should be run. Knowing what's best for everybody is like a financially transmitted disease.

To be fair, I did the same thing with spiritualizing poverty in the early 2000s when we were just getting started and didn't have any money. And to be fair (again), I have a deep-seated and probably sinfully wary response toward Christians with a lot of money. Something that I know is sinful and stupid but still do is measuring my own worth against theirs based on finances. And I almost always lose. Why do I do this? And why are Christians weird about money?

I mean, there's gotta be some kind of right and happy medium between being obsessed with money (like the world), obsessed with money but dipping that in a thin veneer of spirituality (the Mamsey disciples), and poor. Right?

BP I don't know how anyone doesn't have a weird relationship with money. I think the question is just whether or not you realize it. I was hyperaware of money from an early age. That's what happens when your dad preaches about "wartime lifestyle." For those who aren't familiar, this is the mindset that since life is a spiritual battle, we should all live like the patriotic housewives of the 1940s who eschewed all luxuries for the sake of the war efforts until their men got home. It means there are no casual expenditures and having the nagging sense that every single one *could* have been cheaper. And it means being aware of every single dollar all the time—at least, that's how it manifested for me. I didn't learn to budget properly until I was well into adulthood, but I *knew* how many dollars I did or did not have at any time.

To make matters weirder, I was never sure if we were poor folks who should have been rich, rich folks who lived poorer than we were, or just plain old middle class. My dad was a pastor, which was evidence that maybe we were poor. He wrote lots of books that people liked, which indicated maybe we were richer than I thought. Over time our church grew, and I learned that megachurch pastors are often rich (a whole other weird thing), so maybe we were that? And I learned that my dad gave away every dollar he earned from book royalties or speaking honorariums, so maybe we weren't rich. We applied for financial aid when I went to Wheaton College (another superaffluent place), so maybe we weren't rich. They didn't give us any, so maybe we were richer than I thought.

College didn't clarify matters because Wheaton was just as polarized. I was friends with missionary kids who depended on financial aid and meal plans and stayed on campus during most holidays. And I knew private-plane-traveling, third-home-in-the-Caribbean kids for whom misplacing a Patagonia jacket was like dropping a quarter. Again, I was somewhere in the middle, though closer to the missionary kids. And I think being in the middle meant I always compared myself—better off than some and jealous of others. That has been a hard thing to grow out of, especially because hyperawareness of money and love of money are kissing cousins.

RM I'm so happy we get to chat about money given that it's not that big of an issue for society anymore and most of us have a superhealthy relationship with it.

My experience growing up was...well, I don't know, it was all I knew, just like everyone else in the world. But we were one of those families who looked like we had money but were actually struggling like heck. Here's why.

Before FedEx and UPS kinda ruled the world, my dad, one John F. Martin, started a local trucking company in the early '70s and by decade's end had experienced some measure of success. During this time of plenty (and I was so little, I couldn't really benefit from it anyway), we moved to this poshy, rural haven in Southern California called Carbon Canyon. The Canyon was a commuter paradise. Think of it as an off-the-beaten-path mountain getaway 30 minutes south of Orange County where all the houses were on one-acre estates and had long driveways that overlooked an embarrassingly expensive golf course. To live in the Canyon meant something to people who were caught up in the not really hustle and bustle of Orange County. What it communicated was that you were someone who refused to be held hostage by the social hypocrisy of OC and wanted a more tranquil and wealthy environment to raise your kids and the $1 million worth of horses you were likely going to buy for them. Two problems ensued in the Martin household:

1. Dad's business started to tank during the recession that hit in the early '80s.

2. Dad was the least frugal guy you'd ever meet (which is one of the things I loved about my dad and why I struggle with frugality), so the words "broke" and "Martin" became synonymous. Like Brokartin.

Of course, nobody would have guessed that there was anything wrong if you pulled a hard right into the palatial Western Hills Estates and saw our custom-built McMansion shining like a beacon on the top of the hill. But you would have been slightly clued in had you walked inside during the summer and noticed that it resembled Heat Miser's lair because the air conditioner hadn't been running for weeks. You may have further wondered what was going on when the sheriff drove up our long driveway one morning and repossessed the station wagon, which was a downgrade from the 12-passenger Ford Econoline that we had to tragically let go.

My point is that our theology of money is inherited from our parents. In church circles, it seems like you run into the more frugal types (who oddly seem the most vocal). Of course, there's nothing wrong with frugality, except when generosity comes in short supply as a result. EDITOR'S NOTE: Including generosity of spirit, as in not judging those who handle their money differently than you do. And I think that's where I struggle. I'm not a frugal person, but does that mean I lack stewardship? Maybe, but it doesn't automatically mean that I'm generous either. The book of Proverbs has some things to say about these topics, last time I checked.

TK You guys both make great points. It's easy to be a materialist—like Pipe said, being hyperaware of money—while clothing it in the persona of frugality. That's probably where many church people end up, if not just ending up in the kind of megachurch context that just openly celebrates it. Like Ron said, the Bible has so much to say about this, which conveys its importance, yet I never feel like I'm "doing" it quite right. I feel like I'll probably end up like John F. Martin…enjoying it in the moment but never quite able to save enough of it to provide the "security" my heart thinks it desires, but it is that selfsame security that tempts me not to rely on the Lord for my daily bread.

Another thing I struggle with is seeing the way many churches and church people (and Christian colleges) literally drool all over themselves when somebody with a little bit of cashish walks through the door. Those people often end up on boards or in positions of leadership that they probably shouldn't have. EDITOR'S NOTE: Often this happens because lots of cashish means the potential for large donations. Large donations lead to lots of influence. Or should we say, leverage.

Real talk here: This (money—acquiring it, saving it, etc.) is probably the single greatest part of adulthood I hate the most. For many years I (probably naively) viewed talent and work ethic as the greatest investments I could make. I figured that if I put a lot of hooks in the water work-wise, it would all work out. But one of the gifts of adulthood (painful, but still) is just the stark realization that there's really a ceiling on my talent. I mean, I think I'm good, but probably not good enough to make millions. This is okay, and I'm no longer bitter or upset about it. But it's also why this semester, I literally have an undergraduate finance student teaching me about investing. Sigh.

RM Scripture is not incredibly subtle about money. It never says, "Burn all the money"; it says don't let a love for money burn inside of you. The thing is, I always think, "I don't really love money," but it sure occupies some significant space in my head. Is there a way that we spiritualize money that is actually masking a subtle (okay, not so subtle) greed at work in our hearts? In other words, who has more "issues" with money, the person who unabashedly does everything in their power to accumulate more, or the one who's constantly worried that they don't have enough? My problem with money is that it takes up too much real estate in my head due to worrying about it rather than the worship of it. I think. I mean, I have been known to lie to myself on occasion. But what's the difference in the end, you know?

BP I'm not totally sure how the following thoughts combine into a coherent idea (maybe they don't), but these are some observations about money and the church that leave me stumped and uncomfortable. And I think some of them even tie in with what y'all have been saying.

Money is absolutely a status symbol. When we find out how much someone else earns, we cannot help but view them in a new light. We might be impressed. We might be disappointed. We might be jealous. We might gain respect for them. We might judge them for how we perceive their use of money.

This leads me to the second thought: We can't help but judge people about their money. We pity them. We resent them. We think they should use their indeterminate income differently. ("They bought a boat? Slave Whamsey would not approve. I wonder if they had a 'boat money' envelope.") And we're jealous even as we judge.

And of course the church loves capitalism. "Get rich so you can give a lot." In itself, it's good advice, at least for the church coffers. The problem is all of the above words we have written: A lot of money is a temptation (see camels traversing eyes of needles). Our propensity when we earn a lot is to keep a lot and spend a lot.

But beyond this, we have come to see capitalism as a moral virtue, at least in the white evangelical church. There is a sort of heavenly glow around the successful businessmen; we cede power in the church to those who cut big checks, and we assume that a seat in the C-suite is a qualification for eldership. In the end, we often end up with a board of directors or trustees rather than, you know, elders who shepherd a church.

On the other hand, there is a pendulum-swing toward justification-by-poverty, sort of a bastardization of the wartime lifestyle. As if not having money is inherently more righteous than having it (pay no mind to the sinful heart behind the curtain). Underemployment is a fruit of the spirit, and the patchouli wafting off their dreadlocks and unwashed vintage T-shirts is the aroma of Christ. (And as an added bonus, Birkenstocks even kinda look like Jesus's sandals.)

I'm reminded of Jesus saying not to let your right hand know what your left hand is doing when you give. So little good comes from being aware of anyone's money. I mean, very little good comes from me even being aware of my *own* money—regardless of how much it is. How can we, individually and in the church, lose some awareness of money for everyone's sake?

TK I think we can probably stop fast-tracking rich guys right into positions of leadership and stop convincing ourselves that rich guys are going to be amazing friends just because we want to use their yachts. I mean, the board of directors at your Christian college could probably do with one fewer rich guy and one more normal guy with unique insights. Can a rich guy be a good leader? Of course. Are all rich guys leadership material? They are not.

It occurs to me that the church is all about "multigenerational" discipleship. We should probably be similarly about "multisocioeconomic" discipleship. It might be interesting. We might learn some stuff from each other.

Though I'm probably jaundiced by the fact that some of my most uniformly miserable experiences as a Christian writer have taken place when working with rich "Christian" dudes.

RM Fascinating concept, Big T. It makes me think that ideally, this kind of socioeconomic diversity should be represented on a board of elders, for example, and it might be (it is at our church). But when do we ever let someone who makes a small to modest income and manages his finances well ever speak into upper-level financial matters in a church setting? Not trying to be too literal here, but it's the moneymakers who seem to get the biggest seats at the money table (and you better believe I almost typed in "money changers' table," but it probably didn't make enough sense).

To Pipe's point, a church will typically preach a sermon series on money when giving is down, but I wonder how much more valuable it would be to preach one when giving is up. To remind people that (1) their worth is not in what they own and (2) richness toward God is the ultimate aim behind stewardship. It seems like this should be something that informs our doctrine way more than it does.

BP Man, I love the concept of multisocioeconomic discipleship, or at least leadership. It would make such a difference to have a church that honored and looked up to elders and other leaders who are blue-collar working stiffs with profound character and love of Jesus. When we elevate rich dudes to leadership, the implication is that wealthiness is next to godliness, and even beyond that, that wealth reflects God's favor and presence.

It seems to me that the church (here's looking at you, fellow pastors) needs to say a lot more and a lot less about money. Frankly, we probably don't need many more sermon series about giving. But we do need the kind of talk about money that puts it in its place. Money is just a resource. It is a means to something else. Some people have more; others have less. Some people are really clever with it; others are ignorant. Some people have a great plan for theirs, and others wing it. Just like time or talents or energy.

When we, the church, talk about "stewardship" of money, we are usually misguiding people. First, because we use "stewardship" to mean "giving." Second, because we rarely talk about stewarding any *other* resource. Stewardship means being wise caretakers of something that was given to our care; it isn't ours, so we must use it the way the owner (hint: God) wants. Our money was given to us. Our health and vitality were given to us. Our time was given to us. All of it needs to be *stewarded.* I think if we made the shift toward this mindset in our churches, if we discipled and preached this way, much of what is problematic about money would fade.

🅡🅜 Yep, it all comes back to Christian stewardship, which, to narrow it down, means everything we own is not really ours to own. The bottom line is that on this side of glory, money is always going to be a temptation. It's going to be something we have to stay constantly on guard against because our hearts happen to enjoy being ruled by a golden god. Or a green god. Or more accurately, a plastic god with a chip, since I haven't used cash or gold bars for currency in like 47 years. EDITOR'S NOTE: The Christian music industry was a wild place, gold bars and all.

But money hits at the source of our security, and it does it in such a raw and illuminating way. I don't know how many nights my heart begins thumping rapidly in my chest because some financial concern forces its way into the stress chamber of my mind. Where is my theology in those moments? Because I know that although God doesn't promise financial success (sorry, Joel O.), He does promise His faithfulness to provide for my needs. Why is it so hard to believe that?

To layer down a bit, why is it so hard to be content with the needs He's been faithful to provide for me so faithfully all these years? Why do I think that somehow God is not as concerned with my future as I am, as if He is somehow unaware of what I'm going to need at 75, assuming I'm going to outlive every man in my family and make it to that age anyway (sorry this is getting dark)? I have 97 more questions to ask, but they'd be largely rhetorical, since I'm trying to believe and trust that God supplies the ends and the means for the children of man. Speaking of children of man, King Solomon has some good stuff to say in Ecclesiastes (5:18-20) about this sort of thing:

> Behold, what I have seen to be good and fitting is to eat and drink and find enjoyment in all the toil with which one toils under the sun the few days of his life that God has given him, for this is his lot. Everyone also to whom God has given wealth and possessions and power to enjoy them, and to accept his lot and rejoice in his toil—this is the gift of God. For he will not much remember the days of his life because God keeps him occupied with joy in his heart.

THOUGHT LEADERS—NEITHER THINKERS NOR LEADERS

TK Much like "creativity," we've created a cottage industry around making nonleaders feel like they're leaders, because it is sexy and fun to talk about and people can talk about it almost indefinitely. There are a bunch of non-leaders in the leadership industry making bucks off it. That's okay...but doing a bunch of this stuff and reading about it doesn't mean you can lead your way out of a paper bag...until people actually follow you. **EDITOR'S NOTE:** It helps if they follow you to somewhere better than where they are. In much the same way that going to a writer's conference doesn't make you a writer. Actually, writing something makes you a writer, so it follows then that actually leading makes you a leader.

Do people actually follow you in any context? Be honest with yourself. If so, you're a leader. If not, then you probably aren't yet. **EDITOR'S NOTE:** Social media is not such a context. If "following" merely entails clicking a pixel, then it doesn't count.

When I was a freshman in high school, I was a quiet, skinny, shy, mousy little dork in a tough little blue-collar town. The alpha of our team, David Parker—an incredibly handsome, incredibly talented football golden god—took me in. He saw something in me. Taking on Andrew Romine—our other senior alpha—and getting freight-trained by him in practice, to such a degree that my helmet was ajar and my face was bleeding, made me a "made" man in the eyes of those alphas and my coach. That day, at age 14, I became a little dorky baby leader. I came home bruised and scarred and a mess, but my dad respected me, and I knew I had a shot at life. Once I got older and more established, I was always on the lookout for chances to bring young guys in and assimilate them in similar ways—to ease their transition onto the team and assuage their fears—in the same way that Parker did for me. He taught me about leadership in a very tangible way, and honestly, all the poppy leadership stuff comes off as a little ridiculous when compared with sports-related leading, where there is blood involved.

RM I think we've pivoted into this kind of "everybody's a leader" societal thing that is understandable on one hand, but on the other, it also might be blurring our traditional understanding of "leadership." For example, every parent "leads" their kids, but does that automatically identify them as a leader of a particular cultural group or as an "influencer"? Obviously not, but why are we told it's important to think of ourselves as leaders, even if God hasn't given us those gifts?

As a pastor, I've spent lots of heartache wanting someone to become the leader I want them to be only to be disappointed that they just can't fulfill my every wish and desire I have for them. It doesn't mean they don't "lead" anything; it just means they lack this quality of being a "followable" person, and they need an ounce or two of desire to actually want to lead others before anything else. It's a tricky business, this leadership thing. But I don't think we're good leaders if we determine that everyone is a leader, right? Like, everyone didn't lead the children of Israel into the promised land. Everyone wasn't standing on Mount Horeb and getting those non-digital iPads handed to them by God Himself. Everyone wasn't walking around with their face shining like the sun in the Sahara after chatting with the Lord in the tent. Everyone wasn't making fountain drinks out of rocks in the desert. Leadership is given, not grabbed.

BP The term "leader" has gone the way of "courage." It used to be that courage meant doing something sacrificial, acting with decisiveness in the face of fear, and lifting up others or protecting them no matter the cost. It was virtuous. Now "courage" means doing something I'm not sure I want to do. It is mostly self-focused. It was "courageous" to go to counseling. It was "courageous" to have that hard conversation. It was "courageous" to tweet about systemic injustice. While all of these are potentially good, none of them is courageous because there is no significant cost or risk.

Leadership has followed the same path. It used to mean bearing the burden of others, making costly decisions, and having followers who would stay with you at a cost to themselves because they trusted or believed in you. Now it just means declaring yourself a leader (or "influencer") and being loud, or at least pithy, about your ideas.

In both cases, a term that once had meaning, that once *mattered* in the direction and the fabric of society has been diluted to nothing. A "courageous leader" today can simply be a self-centered self-promoter who risks nothing and lifts nobody else up. It's quite literally the opposite of what that phrase used to mean.

And don't get me started on "thought leaders." As far as I can tell, most of the "thought leaders" of today are the winners of a popularity contest, not the people with ideas that have been tried and found true. It is an unofficial democracy of ideas, as if the masses who are making the decisions have ever been discerning. "Thought leaders" of today *are* leading; they're forming how people think and define truth. They're just doing it primarily based on what people want to hear (tickling their ears, to quote one apos-tle Paul) rather than on any merit or truth. So I guess that means they are not thought leaders; they're thought followers.

TK My grandpa was a leader because he was generous. You couldn't pick up a dinner check around my grandpa. He was the guy. The don. Tall, tan, charismatic, good at sports, good at business. People followed him natu-rally. He was generous with his time and generous with his money.

My grandpa was a leader because he told *great* stories with great char-acters and great settings and top-notch humor that didn't sound like flexes. Like all great leaders, he never flexed, but people flexed for him. I heard stories about him that made him sound great from the people who loved and trusted him.

My grandpa was a leader because he wasn't afraid to be the butt of his own jokes. **EDITOR'S NOTE:** Pun not intended, in this case. He was often funny, but he was also often the punch line of his own funny stories. I'm reminded of one he told about a cruise he took once with his best buddy, Butch Shestokas. Because it was the '70s, they were wearing white leisure suits. He and Butch were on their way down to dinner but stopped in the bathroom to take a quick leak. Gramps farted at the urinal but soon dis-covered that not only had he farted; he had accidentally pooped his pants. Gramps loved that story.

My dad is a leader because nobody ever outworked him. I took that into football, then later into writing, and now into teaching. It wasn't compli-cated with my dad as an athlete and later a pilot. He would get into the garage weight room, crank Guns n' Roses, and *grind*. I saw him studying the Bible in the early morning hours. I saw him studying like crazy for his check rides when he was a pilot. He was a workhorse.

My staff needs to see me grinding...writing articles, getting book deals, and caring about the craft. Nobody outreads or outwrites the boy.

Leadership to me—in football and in writing—is very much married to productivity. There's never been an unproductive and lazy football player who was also a leader.

As I think I mentioned on the show and probably at some point in this manuscript, I worked for UPS for a while unloading planes at four in the morning at the Lansing, Michigan, airport. It was a loud, dark, cold, scary job in many ways, and there was this guy on the jobsite that everybody was terrified of named Todd. I got assigned to Todd's team, which was called "Top Deck." It was a fancy nickname we got because we would ride this lift like 30 feet into the air and climb inside a 747 freighter to unload these "cans," which were freight containers and weighed upwards of a couple tons. Because it was Michigan, it was always dark and sleeting. Pretty much the only job requirement of Top Deck was the ability to push and pull large amounts of weight without getting tired. In addition to writing, this is the only other thing in the world I can do well, so it felt like a good job fit.

Anyway, everybody was afraid of Todd because he worked really fast, said almost nothing, and was really intense. On the rare occasions when he said something, it was just to get mad. Todd's sidekick for like a decade was this guy named Danny who was older and quiet and very nice in addition to also being an extremely hard worker. Todd's pet peeve was lazy people, and on the first day, he regaled me with stories about lazy guys that he had run out of Top Deck and/or who had lost fingers or toes to the multiton cans sliding around on these tracks in the plane. I was terrified. Though I soon learned that if you worked really hard and didn't complain—extra points for not saying anything at all—Todd was your closest ally. Armed with this knowledge, we got along great, and (thankfully) nobody got hurt or killed.

Todd was a leader. He got the results he wanted and needed, he encouraged excellence, and he never once wrote on glass, gave me a book to read, asked me to explain my goals, or even cared that I did or didn't have a five-year plan. I kept having to explain to my boss that I *wanted* to stay in the Top Deck team because I really liked working with Todd and Danny.

In the faith realm, I have an amazing pastor at my current church, Cornerstone Community Church in Jackson, Tennessee. Lee is kind, studious, extremely humble, and a great teacher of the word. I can say with all sincerity that I hope he is my pastor for the rest of my life. And though he leads us very well, I don't consider him a "leader" in the traditional sense in that he is so good at leading with a handful of other elders. I don't think I've ever heard him refer to a "leadership" book, in or out of the pulpit.

So there's my take on leadership. Why do you guys think there's such a big emphasis on "leadership" and "thought leaders" nowadays? Is it because it takes the focus off actual leadership and production?

BP Two things come quickly to mind in answer to that question: status and money. And the idea that status leads to money.

"Leader" has become a status, not a measurement of skill or production or sacrifice. We know this because so many people aspire to it and claim it. If leadership was understood rightly, as in all the paradigms you described, Ted, people would shy away. Who wants to outwork everyone with or without credit and be self-deprecating and humble? That sounds *hard*. Leadership as a status is easy...and useless.

But it's also saleable. Faux leadership can be marketed, packaged, pitched, and sold because people really want to hear that they too can get rich by not grinding and being humble. We all want to get paid for being more important than other people.

A striking parallel is the rise of "hustle." When I was growing up, especially in sports, "hustle" meant effort and hard work. It was how a guy like me with middling athleticism could be a varsity starter at anything. I might not be able to run as fast or jump as high, but I could just keep on coming. It was synonymous with grinding.

"Hustle" has morphed into something else though. When people, especially influencer/thought-leader types, talk about hustle now, it is more like a formula or a scheme. "Hustle your a** off for a little while, and you can live this glam life too." "Hustle" no longer describes hard work—it now means schemes and shortcuts. "Work smarter not harder" is the motto, but "smarter" just means less hard (or outsourcing). It is an effort to maximize payoff with as little sweat equity invested as possible. And it's an ego flag to be flown too.

If "leaders" are "hustling," who is benefitting? Who is working hard? Who is sacrificing for the good of other people? Who is quietly going about their business to set an example for others? Who is eschewing credit and simply celebrating results?

It's hard for me to go too far down this road without thinking about Jesus's words: "The good shepherd lays down his life for the sheep" (John 10:11). Shepherds protect, provide, guide, and correct. They work long hours, and their entire responsibility is the health and flourishing of their sheep. So even as they are living, they are laying down their lives. That is the epitome of good leadership. It isn't a hustle. It isn't a status. It's not lucrative. It's no scheme. It's often anonymous and occasionally derided. It's exhausting.

But nobody wants to sign up for that webinar.

RM It's true. The catch-22 of leadership is that the leaders we should be seeking advice from are likely the ones you just described, Pipe. They're not going to have platforms or podcasts, but they are going to model something incredibly Christlike that will probably do more to form you as a leader than any book or webinar ever could. The problem is that this method of leadership development is not marketable, which shows you where we tend to derive our value for leadership. But some of this is unavoidable, isn't it?

BP Ted sort of answered this earlier, but I think it's worth exploring a little more explicitly. What kind of leaders makes us want to follow them?

I'm going to steal Ronnie's line here and say those who have humility. I can follow a leader who isn't self-important. I've seen this exhibit itself in many ways, but a few that come to mind are leaders who...

- take correction and even seek it out from both those at their positional level and those under them;
- give clear rationale, vision, and reason for decisions instead of relying on their authority;
- hand off credit and pass out praise lavishly and by name (and not always to the same few names);
- take the blame as the one responsible when things go sideways;
- treat people as well behind closed doors as they do in public so that the closed-door meeting isn't a threat but an opportunity;
- point to those they learned from and are learning from;
- share responsibility and authority, especially in areas they aren't as good in as other teammates; and
- are focused not on leading itself but primarily on a mission or objective.

But I need the leader to be confident and competent too. It's *really* hard to follow a leader when you could do their job better than they can. Or when they aren't sure of what they're doing. I don't ask much affirmation from leaders, but I need clarity and to trust them. I need to know *why* I am doing what I'm doing, where it's taking us, and what vision they have.

It helps me a lot when a leader can balance friendship with authority too, which is hard to do. I want to be able to crack jokes, grab drinks, and clown around with them. Then follow their lead through difficult situations. In fact, it helps me follow their lead when I actually like them as a person.

(Let the reader understand, everything I've written here requires actual leadership, the kind that involves hard work and sacrifice. Not thought leadership. Not influence. But real skin and blood and sweat and tears in the game.)

What about y'all?

TK This is a really strong list, Pipe, and mine would be similar, I think. That said, I'm still hung up on this idea that there's almost zero correlation with people I've met who have an abiding interest in leadership being actual good leaders.

Similar to humility, which is something we're kind of throwing around as a good word (it is) but not really defining a whole lot. In the Bible, growing in humility went hand in hand with being exiled, imprisoned, or stricken in some way (thinking Paul, David, and others here). Which is to say that real humility often comes at a steep cost that, if pressed, none of us would really say we want but that, at some level, all of us may have walked through some version of in the past.

I'm also having a hard time with the fact that most of what we do in a modern context—tweeting, podcasting, generalized humblebragging, and self-aggrandizement—stands directly at odds with both leading well and being humble.

Similarly, leadership ability—and even leadership opportunity—in the Bible was almost always bestowed, was almost never striven for, and in many cases, was entered into with fear and trembling (thinking Moses here but others too).

I'll need Ron to put a positive spin on this to close the chapter, but where I'm landing is that these (leadership opportunities and humility) are things both that can be prayed for and in which the Lord's provision of is paramount. Meaning that if I have managed to become humble in any way, it's because the Lord has allowed it and ordained it through circumstances in my life. Similarly, if He is for some reason allowing me to lead others, I'm compelled to pray (a) that I won't screw it up and (b) that I can remain humble while doing it.

Experientially, for me at least, leadership has been a lot less glamorous and fun than the books make it sound. It's mostly being available for phone calls or texts at inconvenient times, risking embarrassment, admitting failures, and choosing not to be offended by stuff. None of this is sexy. But we *do* need people who are good at it in the church and in other contexts. Ultimately, I think the best leaders are servants, and being a servant doesn't necessarily help sell books.

RM This last point is so big, Big T. Even people with leadership platforms (which God grants to some) can and should encourage the leadership model that Jesus designed, even though it's a model that's never really "taken off."

Leadership is like anything else in that those who do it don't mind if it's as enjoyable and lucrative as humanly possible. The problem is that if the aim of leadership is greener pastures and greater platforms, then we're ultimately leading ourselves instead of giving ourselves away to others, which is the heart of true, Christ-centered leadership.

The mark of a humble leader will be seen in the fear and trembling in which they work out their salvation. What I mean is that humble leaders enjoy leading because they see themselves first and foremost as people who are being led. Their ego doesn't have time to inflate because Christ is being inflated over infantile and immature desires to "lord it over" and "exercise authority over" others. In a way, the greatest leaders don't identify with being "leaders" as much as people who are being led by Jesus to lead others to Jesus. Any other kind of leadership is bad for our sanctification.

AT THE MOVIES

TK Imagine being a sheltered, evangelical eighth grader in the Midwest in the 1990s and being uncool. It's easy for me to imagine this because this was me. **EDITOR'S NOTE:** It was also Barnabas, just slightly later in the '90s, and Ronnie, just a few hundred miles west. I had a cool friend, Bernie, who had access to girls. He called me one day and asked if I wanted to go on a double date with some Montpelier girls. Montpelier is the next town over from mine and isn't nearly as cool and exotic as its name would suggest. I said yes, of course, because I wanted to be the kind of guy who went on dates.

Anyway, one of the girls' moms picked us up and took us into Muncie to watch a movie called *The Silence of the Lambs*, which to this day may be the most depraved thing I've viewed with my eyes. What I wanted to do was run out of the movie theater crying, but I instead just picked a point on the wall, just adjacent to the screen, and stared at that point, praying that the movie would end quickly. It was an awful experience.

Because I have a reputation now as someone who likes movies, I'm often tasked with choosing them in group settings. A church-type mom asked me recently to pick out a movie for their family to watch—basically something great and engaging and well written but with little to no "grittiness" or "content." I chose *Back to the Future* for her because it's '80s, super fun, super rewatchable, and may actually be the perfect movie. I forgot, of course, the whole Biff-Tannen-date-rape scene in the third act, which, upon further reflection, was a bit of a deal. Anyway, she hated the movie. Tough. **EDITOR'S NOTE:** The Oedipus complex undertones likely didn't help the situation.

That said, I have a theory of filmmaking that says that in order for a movie to be good, it has to have equal parts "total depravity of man" and "created in God's image." Think about it. Movies that are all "total depravity"—and I'm thinking of movies like any early Tarantino (*Reservoir Dogs*), early Guy Ritchie,* early Guy Ritchie knockoffs (read: *Boondock Saints*†), almost anything with Laura Linney,‡ or *The Silence of the Lambs*—are really hard to watch because they feature no redemptive arc and no characters who are anything other than despicable in every way. For me, it's just too much depravity to stew in for two hours.

Conversely, films that are all puppy dogs and ice cream, like *Facing the Giants* (or anything else by the Kendrick brothers), are equally difficult to watch, but for completely different reasons. They start with a "message"

---

* These movies are catnip for a certain kind of guy who wants to be tough, wants to be European, wants to look cool while smoking, and doesn't want to look stupid in a leather jacket.

† The hardcore *Boondock* guys (read: my friend Zach) are gonna kill me for that take, but it's just that in my moral economy, they never did enough good to make up for that cat getting shot (spoiler: A cat gets shot).

‡ She's a great actor, but almost all of her movies contain some combination of gut-wrenching adultery, substance abuse, and somebody working in academia but making it look grim and depressing.

(God is good, porn is bad, whatever) and reverse engineer a usually crappy and paper-thin story with flat, one-dimensional characters.

All of which to say, probably all of my favorite shows and movies, with the exception of *Hoosiers** (basketball, Indiana, Gene Hackman) and *You've Got Mail* (the perfect rom-com), are "gritty" and have "some content." **EDITOR'S NOTE:** For those who did not grow up in evangelical conservatism, "gritty" and "some content" are codes for violence, profanity, nudity, and sex.[†] I mean, my favorite show of all time, *Cheers*, was about a borderline sexual predator (Sam), a high-functioning alcoholic (Norm), and an insufferable bloviating egomaniac (choose Diane or Frasier). And *Cheers* feels downright quaint and wholesome compared to the dreck that's on today.

The nonexhaustive list of my favorite gritty movies includes *Die Hard, Jerry Maguire,* any late-model Tarantino, *Moneyball,* any Wes Anderson, and even all the screwball '80s and '90s comedies that came out back when it was still legal to be funny.

Even though my conscience is largely seared on this matter (as evidenced by the above list), we still occasionally shut shows off. We couldn't do *Game of Thrones,* which in addition to the soft-core pornography was a nonstarter for me because I can't care about anything with a fake dragon in it. Ditto for space. If it's in space and isn't *Apollo 13,* I couldn't care less. We tried a really interesting time-travel series called *Outlander* recently, which we had to tap out of because each episode featured a very graphic and ridiculous seven-minute sex scene that we both laughed at and felt guilty about watching. But we loved *Hunters,* which is the very definition of "gritty."

---

* KK played the soundtrack to this for me on a recent car trip, and within a few bars, I was weeping uncontrollably due to the grandeur of the soundtrack and those opening shots of Indiana in the fall. God's country.

† By which we mean just nudity and sex.

As I tell my students often when this stuff comes up or when it's time to screen a movie for my screenwriting course, I really care deeply about protecting their innocence, and wish I could reclaim some of mine.

What about you guys? How do you handle it?

RM Baby, I need to go back to the future on this one a bit, and by "back to the future," I mean back to the 1980s, which was the decade that everyone in the '50s thought was going to introduce the future, but what it actually gave us was a rash of indoor malls, Cyndi Lauper records, neon-orange Reeboks, and Molly Ringwald movies (which was kind of an awesome future, by the way). But 1980s church culture was when we saw the battle lines drawn between the "sacred and the secular" in regard to all things pop culture. So being part of a family who practiced Christian values meant that there was going to be a supersharp divide between what the world had to offer and what, well, James Dobson had to offer (who embodied the kind of godly guardrails that were necessary for parents to raise their kiddos right). All to say, it was fairly clear what was and was not allowed under this religious regime. Yeah, I just said "regime."

So anyway...without breaking down all the good-time fundamentalist vibes that resulted from that era, the '90s saw a pretty seismic shift taking place. I know this firsthand because I was part of this shift on some scale as an artist signed to the hugely influential Christian record label Tooth & Nail Records. Basically, a new freedom to enjoy non-Christian art was being explored by Gen Xers who saw that not all art being created by non-Christians was inherently bad. Sure, discernment was needed, and parents seemed to be using some of it, which was a progression from the flurry of *no*s that would have typically come pouring from their lips a decade earlier (if even that).

Moving forward to where Big T so eloquently began this chapter, we're at a place where discernment has turned into whether you have the time to binge-watch *Game of Thrones* and still be a responsible parent, or get the right amount of physical rest, or not become too lazy. Discernment as a whole has been recast as something far less to do with character development and Christlikeness than it is doing what's best for you and making sure you don't judge others. Now, let's keep the "not judging others" thing alive here, because that's actually godly discernment, but is it fair to say that we've shelved this idea of discernment in favor of not falling back down the legalist pit of despair that we've become rightly sensitive to?

BP Discernment took quite a beating from a certain brand of bloggers, seemingly all spawned in the early 2000s out of that legalistic regime you described. It became synonymous with hating fun things, insulting fellow Christians, and generally giving no grace. I think it's fair to say we have largely discarded discernment. Or maybe it's more accurate to say we think we have "moved beyond it" as if we are too mature and worldly-wise to need it anymore.

At its best, discernment is weighing what is good for us and what is not and making decisions accordingly, the godly character you described, Ronnie. (Akin to what the Bible calls "wisdom.") And Christians have become much better about doing this with vitamins, essential oils, and educational philosophies than with morals and media consumption. We will spend months researching what Montessori school to send our newborn infant to in four years and then turn around and binge-watch a show with more sex in it than we had on our honeymoon. So yeah, I'd say discernment isn't having its finest day in the church.

TK Yeah, we've sacrificed discernment on the altar of looking cool. Or rather, not wanting to look uncool. And with prestige television really kind of replacing movies in the cultural milieu* and being the new home of no-context '80s nudity (i.e., nudity in a show for absolutely no reason), there are more opportunities to exercise discernment—or at least look for the kind of elite storytelling moment that appears in a more wholesome (or at least a nondark) context.

Speaking of…Tom Hanks, who you could argue invented secular wholesomeness and may be America's de facto secular pastor. My wife and I went to a movie at a local theater the other night. It's something we haven't done in a while for obvious reasons, which isn't to say that we were being especially noble or thoughtful about others (vis-à-vis COVID) but more to say that it wasn't an option.

We saw the new Tom Hanks picture *News of the World,* in which Hanks plays a former Civil War soldier who now travels from town to town reading newspapers out loud to people. You had me at Western, newspapers, and Tom Hanks, due to me being a middle-aged white man.

Once we sat in our seats, we realized that the adjacent theater was showing *Wonder Woman 1984,* which is three hours of stuff exploding and people shouting at each other. The audio from that movie was bleeding over into our quiet little dialogue-driven Western and, in doing so, ruining it. Then I did something I never do: I talked to the manager. For an introvert and a people-pleasing Midwesterner, complaining to a manager is anathema to me.

What I soon discovered was that the manager of this particular theater was like nine years old. Not really, but it seemed like it. EDITOR'S NOTE: For our younger readers, at about 35 years old, everyone under the age of 25 reverts to "child." He was really young because, in my mind, it seemed like "theater manager" is a job for a respectable 35-year-old. EDITOR'S NOTE: In the '80s, Ted's heyday, this was actually true. In his presence, I felt like an

---

* Solid McCrackian vocab flex there.

85-year-old man asking him to turn down the volume on the fun popcorn flick playing adjacent to the old-man movie I was watching. I was able to show him (in a way that I'm sure was not condescending) that the doors of movie theaters were designed to be closed when the movies are playing and that doing so would, like, hold a lot of the noise in. He seemed really pleased to make this discovery, and I hoped that I handled the interaction in a way that would make Tom Hanks proud.

Watching Tom Hanks is, of course, just a tangible reminder of all the ways you're failing as a man. By reeking of credibility, calmly being in control of every situation he's in, running Fox Books, wooing Kathleen Kelly, landing Apollo 13, surviving a deserted island, doing that movie about AIDS way before wokeness was even a thing, imploring you to be his neighbor, managing an all-women's pro baseball team (EDITOR'S NOTE: Just ignore his moderately functioning alcoholism in this one), soldiering in a variety of contexts, and even getting COVID before everybody else and riding it out with his trademark charm/aplomb, Hanks is the [pick one: pastor, dad, high school football coach] you never had.

In the same way that TED Talks are "sermons" for secular people, it occurred to me that, for many, Hanks is their de facto secular "pastor"—always waiting in the wings to gently guide them into the right frame of mind about [insert any issue here from eschatology to space travel to politics]. He took this title belt from Oprah when she relinquished it a few years ago. Vaguely inspirational, distant but somehow knowable, your fake pastor Tom Hanks will never tell you that you're wrong, will always take you for ice cream after the game, and will always encourage you to take a flier on meeting that girl in the Empire State Building to whom you've been writing clandestine letters.

Of course, thinking about this made me thankful for my real pastor because he is similarly kind, genuine, helpful, knowledgeable, funny, and humble—but with the additional and not small caveats that he knows *me* well and (much more importantly) knows Jesus and the Bible. He would actually, thankfully, be quick to point out what I was doing wrong but also be just as quick to point me to my Redeemer. He would, and does, do the same for himself from the pulpit. He doesn't judge me for the grossness in my heart, but he loves me enough not to let the sin go unchecked.

In 2021, even mentioning the idea of sin is a near-revolutionary and somewhat scary act. But I need it. Even more than I need to be lulled into a false sense of security by the world's greatest movie pastor.

BP What's crazy is that Tom Hanks has assiduously avoided movies rife with "grittiness" and "some content." So even the discerning folks can appreciate him.

Something came to mind as I read your description of Tom as pastor (he's so likable, I feel like I can just use first names here), and it was the idea of movies as sermons. It used to be that moral conservative talking heads decried the influence Hollywood was having on America's youth, turning us all into narcissistic, profane, sex-crazed punks who were numb to violence. Those voices got shouted down and moved to Internet backwaters, homeschool conventions, Grand Rapids, and Colorado Springs. We ignored them because they sounded like shrill doomsday-naysaying kooks.

But...it sure seems like America is full of narcissistic, profane, sex-crazed punks who are numb to violence. Or maybe it's full of the offspring (spawn?) of such folks. Were the conservative kooks right? Did the denim-jumper crowd see something the rest of us missed? Have movies and TV discipled us into sin?

RM I think the denim-jumper crowd was...wait for it...right (literally and figuratively). But they were wrong by being woefully unaware of how *they* had been influenced by *who* and *what* had discipled *them*. When I say *unaware,* I mean they were unaware by assuming that *whoever* and *whatever* had discipled them was somehow "better" than the *who* and the *what* that were potentially discipling their kids. If you're bored, a brief survey of the religious-political landscape that emerged in conservative evangelicalism during the golden years of 2016–2020 should aptly illustrate my point.

What's funny is that my dad (a nonhippy boomer) always said things like "At least in the old movies, they would leave things to your imagination, but now they just show it all." Of course, being the son of former navy man John F. Martin meant I was probably *not* going to get into a philosophical convo with him about the sinister nature of the imagination and how even old Hollywood required a Christian to take every thought captive. Of course, if you compare *Gone with the Wind* ('30s) to *Fatal Attraction* ('80s), there were some marked differences, especially if you rated sexual promiscuity much higher on the no-no list than, say, racism. Which you did. **EDITOR'S NOTE:** The cultural acceptance, or ranking of evils, has definitely been reversed in recent years. The fully clothed antebellum South is now far more sinister and hated than explicit nudity or fornication in the broader public's opinion. Is this ranking system a way for us to conveniently ignore some sins by focusing on others?

All this to say, the movies and media from my parents' era produced a generation of *somethings* that, although different than the *somethings* it produced in my generation, is still *something* decidedly antithetical to the gospel. The point is, do we recognize it or do we ignore it? Do we think the sins of the next generation we're absorbing are somehow more evil and dangerous than the ones we conveniently absorbed? More than anything, I want to be aware of what's influencing me and then take appropriate action when I realize it is.

And then, I don't know, repent or something.

TK Pipe, to your point about "conservative kooks" and the "denim-jumper crowd" being right: I think they actually were/are. At the end of the day—and maybe this is a function of being older, straight, Baptist, and white and therefore patently uncool anyway—I think I'd rather be uncool with a clean conscience than cool and guilty. What's more, being cool and causing a "little one to stumble," whether it's a student or my own kids, is something that keeps me up at night. I mean, I guess I'd rather be on the outside of the *Game of Thrones* cultural conversation (which, by the way, is already over) than be on the inside of it and causing myself (or someone else) to stumble.

I would posit, as a "Christian" movie done well, the "Christian" movie of my youth: *Chariots of Fire*. I scare-quoted "Christian" because this didn't come out on a Christian label and to my knowledge wasn't made by Christians, but it was about a Christian and was very Christian in terms of the themes and values it explored, and it explored them at a *very* high level in terms of script, budget, and character development. If Christians could be about the business of making movies at or near this level consistently, I think we'd have a lot to be proud of.

As much as it pains me to say this, I think I'd rather be with the denim-jumper crowd on this one* than to be the kind of cool, jaded, hard-hearted hipster† who has consumed everything but loves Jesus less because of it.

BP In the tradition of all good Baptists, I think I just rededicated my life

---

* My twentysomething self would be mortified by my fortysomething self ceding this point.

† We've really failed by writing an entire movie chapter and not mentioning Brett McCracken, who is our favorite aesthete and TGC movie critic who also went to Wheaton College with Piper. McCracken has argued passionately that Terrence Malick's *Tree of Life* is a good movie, about which he is wrong. Malick's *Tree* is a good movie if what you're trying to do is impress people, conversationally, about movies and make yourself look smarter in the process. It is the movie version of Radiohead in that it is exclusively for smart people and isn't a whole lot of fun.

to Jesus again after reading what y'all wrote. Seriously, though, that was some wisdom.

In my lifetime, I think I have expended more effort creatively rationalizing the consumption of movies and shows rife with content and grittiness (i.e., gore and '80s boobs) than I have in any other creative venture. I have expounded upon the character arcs, the cinematography, the artistic value, the redemptive elements, the relative morality of violence/profanity versus nudity, and even the necessity of sex to the plotline. **EDITOR'S NOTE:** Sex is, in fact, essential to everyone's plotline. But that doesn't mean it's for public consumption.

When I was in college, I probably drank four to six Cokes per day and was convinced that the best time to eat a two-pound steak burrito was after midnight. I would put down half a dozen Krispy Kreme donuts in a sitting like it was nothing. And I never gained weight. But I wasn't healthy, or at least my habits weren't, but it didn't matter to me because I could explain away potential ill effects. I found out the cost of this when I got an office job and promptly put on about 30 pounds.

I think the same has been true in my consumption of gritty, content-filled movies. The cumulative effect wasn't visible for a long time. I explained away all the potential costs. But what it all added up to has been a pile of mental images I wish I could do without and, well, not loving Jesus more. I don't know that it's directly made me love Him less—I haven't given my soul to the idols of sex or violence or avarice. But it's taken my eyes off what and who matters most and decreased my enjoyment of Jesus by distraction at the very least. It was a lot of effort and hours expended on making myself feel better about stuff that, at best, made me spiritually flabby.

Actually, this is all a gross understatement. I struggle to remember last week's sermon text. I hesitate when I recite my children's birthdays. I occasionally get my number of siblings wrong. But I don't struggle to remember nude scenes. In fact, they come to mind unbidden. And guess what, it's not because of their cinematography. So what my rationalizing added up to was not an additional 30 pounds that were hard to shed, like Coke and burritos gave me. It added up to a spiritual parasite I am still trying to kill.

Before I get too far into this sermon, let me pause and say I am *not* about to don my denim jumper and start to finger wag. That would have been like taking up CrossFit and going Paleo to lose those 30 pounds. Both would be extreme responses that would drive everyone around me nuts. But something had to change; I needed some way to starve the parasite. Some standards had to shift. Y'all mentioned repentance and loving Jesus more. Those are the foundational standards for any Christian. But what does that look like in our media consumption?

RM I mean, that's the question, isn't it, Pipe? We have a relationship with media on a completely different level than we did 10, 15, or 20 years ago. Back in the day, media consisted of movies, music, television, news channels, and talk-radio shows, but most of those things were typically consumed in bite-sized portions (not saying we didn't have media consumption problems, obvi). But it was likely not something that ruled our lives the way social media does today. I mean, look, I don't care how much you claim to be on Facebook, Instagram, Twitter, or TikTok, the fact is that your phone is a major contributor to your lifestyle. There was a time when none of us were "checking" anything in between breaks at work, during conversations with friends, in our downtime during the day, or in our spare minutes between literally every activity we involve ourselves in over the course of our day-week-month-year. Our devices have become security blankets that we clutch on to for dear life while we suck our thumbs like a bunch of Linuses, fearing our lives might become devoid of all meaning if we are ever separated from them. It's a dilemma, but even as I type this, I know that I can't/won't simply "get rid of my phone" or "get off social media."

To laser in on your question, Pipe, any kind of consumption that moves our spiritual health meters into the red of overindulgence needs to be considered and discerned. I really do think this is where some of the spiritual disciplines help us immensely in reshaping and reordering our desires. Anytime we consume something over and above a level of enjoyment that's edifying and healthy, we need to ask what kind of spiritual void we're trying to fill.

One of the clichés about touring is that by the end of a tour, your inhibitions are so low that you start eating whatever is lying on the ground. You know how horrible you feel, and you know how much better you would feel if you would just eat healthier food and moderate portion sizes, but the irregular rhythms of touring shift your heart into a state of lethargy. I think media overconsumption can do the same thing. It creates an irregularity in our spiritual rhythms that we *must* use wisdom, discernment, and self-control to stabilize.

Practicing the spiritual disciplines (prayer, reading God's Word, and times of reflection, just to name a few) allows us to experience a particular kind of satisfaction and belonging in Christ that our flesh defaults into seeking through means that are more saccharine (flesh) and less pure cane (Spirit). The thing is, I don't want to be ruled by anything saccharine. It has its place for sure, but what I really want is that pure cane sugar because I've had that stuff, and it's the *stuff*.

CAN CHRISTIANS BE FUNNY?

TK One of my sons has some pretty significant learning issues that can sometimes make it tougher for him to connect with other people. One thing he's *never* had trouble with is laughing at, enjoying, and then flawlessly quoting funny movies with a perfect sense of timing. He is far and away the best in our family at this, which is saying something because I'm also pretty good at it.

For example, my wife will ask him to do something, which he will agree to do with a cheerful heart (usually). Then she'll leave the room, and he'll turn to me and say, "I'm so [redacted] off at my mom right now," which is a toned-down version of an all-timer quote from the stupid Will Ferrell comedy *Step Brothers*. If you're reading this and are easily offended, definitely don't go watch *Step Brothers*. Here's another example. We're in the car, and I indicate that we need to turn left.

Him: "I don't care about righty/lefty," a quote from *Moneyball*, which is on my Mount Rushmore of both Brad Pitt and baseball movies.

Me: "Well, I do."

Humor and the ability to laugh at oneself is a pretty foundational core value in our house, and I'm *really* grateful that my kids not only love the Lord but also manage to have a sense of humor. Ditto for my wife, who will randomly text me *Tombstone** or *Die Hard* memes in order to brighten my day. I'm pretty sure this is in Proverbs 31.

One core value of our day seems to be everybody taking every issue— and in doing so taking themselves—*very* seriously. Here's an example, from the university where I teach.

All Christian colleges unfortunately do a fairly brisk business in producing the kind of guy who hits his senior year and is convinced that he is way too enlightened and cool for Christian college. This guy always takes himself very seriously and is always right about everything, and every conversation is just an occasion to demonstrate that he's read a few pages of Noam Chomsky or to indicate that he heard something very interesting on NPR recently. EDITOR'S NOTE: We like to call this the "Ira Glass Effect." It is usually accompanied by a cardigan, horn-rimmed glasses, and that voice that's almost vulnerable but not quite. As you can imagine, the pandemic was a very rich moment for this kind of guy.

Him, on, like, day three of the pandemic: "Kluck, will you admit that we're in the midst of a *global* pandemic?"

Me: "Look…I'm good at two things in this world: writing and coaching football. I'm terrible at—and frankly pretty disinterested in—everything else. EDITOR'S NOTE: We would like Ted's current employer to know that he is also a passionate and gifted teacher, highly rated by students and peers alike. So I don't know if we're in the midst of a global pandemic.† You should ask someone from biology."

---

* The one where Curly Bill Brocius says "Well…bye" is a personal favorite.

† If you're reading this in 2035 (again, God bless you), as it turns out, he was right…we were in the midst of a global pandemic. Or the greatest PR moment ever foisted on America. Or both?

I wasn't trying to be funny, but everybody laughed anyway. Point being, I don't have to have a comment ready, a position established, or a strongly held belief on everything in the world, which is precisely the lie that social media has fed us. Nobody cares what I think of the pandemic, and what's more, nobody *should* care what a random writer/football coach thinks about it.

Humor can diffuse a lot of awkward situations and make a lot of conversations easier. For example, check out this conversation with another student (and a great friend) about a girl he was trying to date in which I was trying to understand what kind of a person she was and if she'd be good for him. This kid happens to be a fount of NBA knowledge, and we talk about it (the NBA) often.

Me: "If she were an NBA player from the '90s, who would you compare her to?"

He smiles, and his face brightens because I am now speaking his language.

Him: "Probably Thunder Dan Majerle, because she's super good looking* and is only really good at one thing, but that one thing she is great at." **EDITOR'S NOTE:** No offense to the young buck, but this scouting report is sorely lacking. Yes, Dan Majerle was nicely coiffed, tanned, and good looking. And yes he could shoot. But he was also sneaky athletic and dunked on unsuspecting opponents with some regularity. He was also a tenacious defender.

We then wasted an hour comparing all our former girlfriends to NBA players, invoking the names of everybody from Sweet Lou Williams†

---

* I have no trouble admitting that Thunder Dan was a great-looking guy in the '90s. Also, the thing he was great at was shooting threes. Thunder Dan would have killed in the three-and-D era.

† "She's occasionally great but disappears for long stretches at a time."

to Gordon Hayward[*] to Will Perdue.[†] We laughed a lot and both felt better.

My question to you guys is as follows: Do we live in a posthumor society? I mean, most things are off limits due to being offensive, sexist, racist, homophobic, political, religious, or just mean. Also, due to the fact that people take themselves so seriously, is humor even possible?

BP First, Ted, please tell the young man who tried to compare the young lady to Dan Majerle that Kyle Korver would have been a better fit. These comparisons matter. They matter a lot. Especially when gauging the likelihood of a future mate. **EDITOR'S NOTE:** Only conservative evangelicals and David Attenborough when narrating *Planet Earth* use the term "mate."

Now to your questions. I do think humor is still possible. It *has* to be possible because we need it. People need to laugh. We need to laugh a lot, and not alone.

A few years ago when I was going through a divorce and life was just grim, I realized something. I was at risk of losing my sense of humor. This would have meant becoming not morose or mopey but rather mean and biting. Things were so dark and so painful that laughing felt alien sometimes. Things that would have had me in stitches a year earlier almost offended me just by existing. (In other words, I was becoming a lot like Twitter.) Other people's laughter ticked me off because I was so far from that place.

I had to make the intentional decision to hold on to humor. Our podcast was a lifeline. Once a week, I was going to record for 40 minutes with you guys, come hell or high water (thankfully neither occurred for any of us) and no matter how many retreats Ronnie absconded to. And I was

---

* "Beautiful and loves video games."

† "Thick ankles. Ultimate teammate."

going to laugh and make you laugh as well as I could. I was going to make jokes on Twitter, and *not* just at people's expense. I was going to respond in kind to the memes and gifs people texted me instead of being irritated. I was going to go out with friends and really listen to their funny stories so I could laugh along with them. I was going to be silly with my kids and double down on fart jokes and Chris Farley movies. I realized that humor is a defiance of sorts, a stiff-arming of darkness and bitterness.

The world sucks in a million ways, and people are trying to defy all those ways right and left (not entirely a political pun but not entirely not one either). Most of this is through frantic serious offendedness, outrage, and vitriol and taking things *very* personally. But humor is better. Screaming back at the world just makes things louder and more annoying. Laughing in the face of evil robs it of some of its power over us and puts a little steel in our spines. If we can laugh, then things aren't as bad as we fear.

TK Dude, that's super cool about the role the pod played. I didn't know that. Humor has a tension-diffusing quality that I never get tired of and always find compelling in a person. I fundamentally distrust people who can't laugh or can't find humor in things because I think the inability to laugh can often (though not always) go hand in hand with smugness.

There's certainly a time and a place to deal with the "hard issues"—as you certainly did in your life and as we're doing with our kids, sick parents, and so on—but for us, consistently looking for reasons to laugh and things to laugh about together keeps us alive.

Honestly, one of the roles I've always played for the pastors in my life is Guy They Can Safely Laugh With.* I'm currently playing that role for like

---

* This is a vital and underappreciated person in a pastor's life. So much of the ministry is devoted to wading into people's problems. And so many people think the pastor is more ethereally holy than he actually is (since he is neither ethereal nor holy). He needs that guy to breathe easy and laugh with. And with whom he can discretely laugh at others.

four pastors. They can reference movies with me, make fun of NFL/NBA stuff with me, and even say the occasional dirtbaggy thing to me without fear of reprisal. We laugh about stuff at our church. We laugh about stuff in Reformeddom at large. We can laugh about the fact that our services are two-hour marathons while at the same time completely loving them. We laugh together *a lot*. I love playing this role for them because their lives are hard and complicated.

There's this pastor on the staff at our church who, for years, people had insisted was a very funny guy. I had no reason to disbelieve these scouting reports, I just hadn't *seen it*. Our kids are playing on the same middle-school baseball team this year, and the other night at the ballpark, somebody made a passing reference to the fact that megachurch pastor James Mac-Donald allegedly hired a hitman to have somebody whacked. Then there was a pause. And then I said, "Guys, I've really been struggling with that lately. It's been a really stressful time for me, and I actually hired two hit-men this week."

"That's every man's battle, Ted," he replied. "I don't want you walking around in shame and condemnation for that." (Laughter.) He continued, "Listen, I want you to just send me a quick text the next time you feel tempted to hire a hitman." (More laughter.)

So, AOK, if you're reading this (and you're for sure not), you're a funny guy.

RM I do think some topics have reached the point of posthumor no return. Maybe for good reason? There are some distasteful things out there that people have justified making "humorous" commentary on that have thankfully become unacceptable. But good actual humor is acknowledging the absurdities of life and making them known quantities. Which might be the unfunniest description of humor in the history of humor. But what you described with your boy Aaron O'Kelley is my favorite kind of funny.

Taking a very serious topic that is simultaneously absurd and horrific in nature and turning it into something that joins you at the hip with another human being. Could someone be offended by this banter? Of course, but humor can be an offense for those who aren't able to take themselves less seriously. That's not a hit against them—or hitmen in general—it's just saying that humor in and of itself has to be at the expense of something or someone or it's not really, well, humorous.

So in this way, the ability to laugh at ourselves is also a way for us to grow in humility (among other things). Now, I know different personalities find different things funny, but a humorless Christian is and should be an oxymoron. We need to fight for humor, not as a way to offend, but as a way to invite others into the ridiculousness of humanity, which can be an incredibly godly endeavor.

TK I'm gonna defend making fun of people here for a minute. Recently I was at a middle school baseball game, which is an exercise in watching wild pitches and walks for two hours. My son's team is the dorky, weirdo classical school team, and we happened to be playing the rich suburban team (RST) whose uniforms, ballpark, and PA system were New York Yankees–worthy. Keep in mind these are eighth graders. But each RST kid had walk-up music. The whole thing was deeply ridiculous. I was sitting with the dads from our school and being a sore loser, seething (of course) with competitive angst.

The angst manifested in me creating a sort of meta-joke in which I chose walk-up music for our "players" (yes, quotations) and even started playing alternate walk-up music (depressing stuff like the Carpenters and "Release Me" by Wilson Phillips) for RST players. Soon, everybody in our section was guffawing, which made our 15–1 loss go down much easier.

Was I making fun of RST? Yes, I was. Did they deserve it? Yes, they did, for treating middle school baseball like it's the American League Championship Series.

I actually think there are lots of things in our culture that we should be going at, and going at *hard*. The human experience is perhaps as ridiculous as it's ever been right now.

BP I am not sure that humor has to be at someone's or something's expense, even making fun of people. That implies that humor takes more than it gives. It certainly can, but the best humor leaves all parties involved better off in some way. **EDITOR'S NOTE:** Humor is about someone, yes, but not necessarily at their expense. It's not costly if it's received humorously, and being the butt of a joke doesn't have to hurt. On top of that, if someone is in a position of influence, power, or comfort, they're well-shielded against incoming barbs. If we're recording a podcast, and I slip up and say something spectacularly inappropriate or embarrassing or dumb (obviously a hypothetical situation) and you guys laugh (which you should), is that at my expense? Maybe, but it can also be the exact thing I need to get past my verbal face-plant, an opportunity not to take myself too seriously. (Come to think of it, that's sort of the motto of the whole podcast: an opportunity not to take anything too seriously.) It's the difference between humor and mockery.

Humor requires a level of mental resiliency that comes from active minds and thick skin. People have to be able to catch up, catch on, and not get offended. And that is lacking now. When my kids are being little savages to each other, I often tell them, "You can be mean if you're funny."* I don't know if it's good parenting, but what I'm shooting for is laughter

---

* ESPN has produced almost nothing good except live sports in the last decade. But I took this directly from Jalen Rose on his podcast and ran with it. All truth is God's truth, after all, even if it's from ESPN.

rather than destruction. It's an art to insult someone so well that you both laugh. And to be able to laugh when you're insulted means you have a thick-skinned resilience and an active mind. And, of course, when we laugh, it's hard to stay mad or be offended.

I think the hardest part about humor is the balance of taking the right things seriously to the right extent *while* being able to laugh at the absurdity surrounding them at the same time. It's what we have tried to do for the last seven-plus years on the podcast: take Jesus seriously, take our faith seriously, laugh at ourselves, and laugh at the absurdity in so much of Christian (and broader) culture. We get it wrong sometimes, and other times we nail it. When we nail it, we strike the balance between appropriate reverence (for Jesus) and poking at the silliness of His people. **EDITOR'S NOTE:** Also an apt description of this book.

How do y'all strike that balance? And even more importantly, how do you develop the sort of resilient mind, thick skin, and ultimate humility to laugh at yourself?

TK Great question. I think for me, a lot of it has to do with growing up in a decade ('80s and early '90s) where the funniest people were the punchlines of their own jokes. A seminal moment of my high school years was watching Chris Farley's* Chippendales audition video on *Saturday Night Live* and thinking it was hilarious. He was the punchline of his own joke, and what made it funnier was the fact that he was complicit in it at that level. Ditto for David Spade's Richard character in *Tommy Boy*. He was making fun of being a pompous, self-important blowhard and in doing so was laughing at himself. Chevy Chase's willingness to look like such a dork in all the *Vacation* movies is what made him so funny. Every time Will

---

* Farley was a fat guy, which is a thing I'm not allowed to say per 2021 orthodoxy. But he was. And that, along with remarkable agility, was part of what made him funny.

Ferrell takes his shirt off in a movie or sketch, it's the same mindset at work. When he raises up a football jersey in a Zoom video to the Seattle Seahawks and says that his "body is a temple," it's funny because he's a flabby, pasty, middle-aged man. If he was weirdly jacked and self-important and prideful about his body, the joke doesn't work.*

Seinfeld worked because of the implicit understanding that they were all horrible people who had no interest in personal growth or development or living their best lives or being on the right side of any issue. In doing so, they were very funny, and it was a social outlet we all needed. I want to see Kramer slide into a room and drop his cigar down his shirt. I don't want him opining about the redistribution of wealth. I want to hear George Costanza on being short, fat, and bald—I don't want to hear him on sexual politics and gender.

It's reductive to say that we've lost that, but we've totally lost it. Today, who's funny?† Today, a late-night comedy show is all about telling the world why you're smarter than they are and why you're a good person because you're on the right side of literally every issue. We live in a world of Stephen Colbert smugness as comedy, which to me just isn't funny. So as a result, our kids have grown up in the kind of vacuum where they have never seen concrete examples of people laughing at themselves. And so they have no idea how to do it.

RM I just think the ability to laugh at oneself is the baseline for enjoying and participating in humor itself. To see the ridiculousness of how we think,

---

* Precisely why Channing Tatum and Dwayne "The Rock" Johnson are only marginally funny.

† I mentioned this before, but I want to do a minute on Jimmy Fallon here. Fallon has succeeded where all others have failed at being America's favorite straight, white, non-threatening, middle-aged man. He's perfect for YouTube and does the right kind of goofy, moderately funny bits where everyone comes away feeling affirmed and nobody gets hurt.

talk, and act is to verge into the realm of the divine in some ways. There's a reason why we love seeing successful people do ridiculous things, and it's because it reminds us that to be imperfect is to be human and that even a person's laughable imperfections don't have to be a barrier to one's opportunities and possibilities. We're simultaneously fascinated and relieved when a gifted athlete, brilliant writer, talented businesswoman, or accomplished musician assures us that they too are foolish, forgetful, clumsy, weird, scared, obsessed, and stressed about all the same stuff that we are.

Humor helps us increase our humility too, which in turn allows us to cultivate a more compassionate and empathetic (if empathy is allowed anymore) opinion of others that helps level the playing field of life. Seeing another person's foibles should remind me of my own and move me to step off my high and mighty pedestal made of reclaimed barnwood.

There's a woman at our church named Jillian who embodies this better than almost anyone I've ever known. She's always the first to crack up at her little idiosyncrasies and imperfections. Let me say it like this: When Jillian does something ridiculous, her tendency is not to go into a defensive or self-protection mode but to broadcast it to the world. And you know what? Everyone feels comfortable and at ease around her. They also see compassion pouring out from her to all who labor and are heavy-laden.

Which sounds like someone else I know.

BP It's interesting that you would bring up Jesus, Ronnie. I mean, who would have expected that from a man of the cloth? But seriously, it's striking because Jesus isn't often associated with laughter. Or fun. But as I think about it, a guy who could keep 12 young men ranging from political extremists to government flunkies to blue-collar laborers as friends had to be a fun guy, right? I have a hard time getting along with one of those guys at a time (especially the political extremist), and He got 12 of them to start a movement that reshaped the world. I'd guess there was some fun and friendship and laughter involved.

I remember hearing a sermon by (TRIGGER WARNING) Mark Driscoll several years back before he was canceled (which was before "canceled" was a thing) and before we relived his canceling in a massively popular podcast. In it he was talking about how *hilarious* Jesus was, just an absolute hoot. He cited the camel going through the eye of a needle and a couple other not-at-all-funny things Jesus said. See, Jesus was *hilarious*! While the message completely missed in its examples (not an isolated incident), I think Mark was on to something.

Jesus was the kind of man who young men wanted to follow, faithfully, for three straight years. Children loved Jesus. He was known for hanging out with tax collectors and sinners, just a debauched bunch. In fact, the only people who didn't like him were the self-important, self-righteous, legalistic, religious killjoys. The man was a pleasure to be around for every normal person, and it's simply impossible for me to imagine that being the case without humor.

All this to say, I agree with you about self-deprecation being a key to humor. So is a keen eye for absurdity. On the one hand, joking is harder than ever for all the reasons we've written about: sensitivity, political correctness, thin skin, and so on. But we all know people who are guaranteed to make us laugh when we see them. We have groups of friends with whom hilarity is a certainty. Shoot, we've done a podcast for years now that relies heavily on humor, and it works.

It seems that maybe the future of humor is humble humor, a kind that invites others to participate. It takes pleasure in sharing laughter more than in being seen or tearing someone down. It looks in the mirror more than it looks through a magnifying glass. And it revels in absurdity, especially absurdity close to home. This has certainly been our best effort for the past seven-plus years on *The Happy Rant*. We haven't always succeeded, and we've had our share of missteps. (Just read our 1-star reviews.) But we've worked hard not to take ourselves too seriously, to laugh at our Christian-y familial idiosyncrasies, and to revel in absurdities as satire. I think there's good in that because it's a kind of humor that invites people in and has staying power.

RM Is there anything less funny than talking about funny? On behalf of *The Happy Rant* podcast, apologies.

BP I feel like as we wrap this chapter, we owe our readers not only the apology you just gave, Ronnie, but also some recommendations on who makes us laugh. I'll go first:

Nate Bargatze (not gritty)—a stand-up comedian who turns the mundane into hilarious stories.

Jim Gaffigan (not gritty)—a stand-up comedian who loves his family and food and making fun of himself.

Dave Chappelle (very gritty)—a stand-up comedian with incisive, brilliant cultural observations and commentary (but again, very gritty).

Fredrik Backman (mildly gritty)—the author of such quirky, hilarious books as *A Man Called Ove* and *Anxious People*. He writes dark, sad books too, and I think that's why he understands humor and the oddities of human nature.

Steve Martin and Martin Short (moderately gritty)—a comedic genius duo who have been making people laugh since the '70s and are still going strong on both screen and stage.

Dad jokes (only as gritty as you want them to be)—there's no such thing as a bad pun, only people who love puns and people who are wrong.

Craig Johnson (moderately to strongly gritty)—author of the Longmire book series and a master of understated and dry humor and witty banter by endearing characters. His plots are good too.

Conan O'Brien Needs a Friend (moderately to strongly gritty)—Conan's podcast in which he interviews friends, usually other funny people, about anything he wants. It's absurd, rambling, and hilarious.

Chris Farley (moderately gritty)—One of the saddest moments for me was quoting *Tommy Boy* to a group of college students a few years ago and receiving naught but blank stares. Today's generation of kids has completely missed not only a comedic classic of a movie but an apex comedic performer in Farley. His SNL bits were spectacular.

Chris Rock (very gritty)—His special, *Bigger and Blacker,* was my first favorite comedy special. He hasn't aged as well as some comedians, but his observational humor and his manner of delivery still get me.

TK Good idea, Pipe. Here are mine:

Hot Rod starring Andy Samberg (mildly gritty)—This isn't gritty at all and is really a sweet story about love and family and dads and "doing" (as opposed to just sitting around and critiquing). It's also incredibly stupid and fun to watch with your sons who are also middle-aged boys.

Lonely Island videos, also starring Andy Samberg (moderately gritty)—This is an interesting brand of humor because Samberg makes fun of a lot of concepts and people in these videos, but they tend to be concepts and people who we either (a) feel are too powerful already or (b) would all assent to as already ridiculous and therefore fair game (such as '90s R&B guys).

Andy Samberg's face (not gritty)—which is just self-evidently funny.

Bill Simmons in *The Book of Basketball* (moderately gritty)—Nobody has ever written about basketball in a funnier way than Simmons in this book, yet it still totally works as a basketball book (his knowledge is encyclopedic, which is kind of the point of this book), and it also works as a book that is reverent about basketball (while also making fun of it).

Chris Farley as a bus driver in *Billy Madison* (moderately gritty)—I'd watch a whole movie about this character...probably multiple movies. It's funny because he stands in for every frustrated authority figure who has ever gotten sick of his lot in life or being around kids. Meaning, every dad, and me most of the time as a dad.

Bill Murray anytime he plays a burned-out, disaffected middle-aged guy (moderately gritty)—Again, I think I relate to these characters, but they are funnier to me than early-career Murray.

Michael Richards as Kramer in *Seinfeld* (mildly gritty)—Kramer anytime he lights a cigar, Kramer attending Yankees fantasy camp, Kramer when he finds the *Merv Griffin Show* set, and Kramer pulling girls way out of his league are all examples of this.

Tina Fey in *30 Rock* (mildly gritty)—She serves as the butt of all the jokes about uptight, self-congratulatory, bleeding-heart, artsy hipster liberals in the media business.

Alec Baldwin in *30 Rock* (mildly gritty)—He serves as the butt of all the jokes about rich, self-congratulatory, stuffed-shirt, greedy conservatives in business in general.

Tracy Morgan in *30 Rock* (mildly gritty)—He's on my Mount Rushmore of people who are funny when they take their shirts off (also Farley, Farrell, and Dennis Rodman while being ejected from games). He is also one of only a handful of people on the planet who made it okay to laugh about race stuff occasionally.

Adam Sandler, Steve Martin, and Jack Black doing music (mildly gritty)—Music people are among the most self-important people on the planet, and seeing these guys do music for humor always works for me.

CONFERENCES, WHY?

TK It feels wrong somehow for me to start this chapter given that we have Conference Man right here in our midst. That said, I'm not a big conference guy, but I want to understand it more.

To me, especially in the Christian realm, it feels like an invitation to listen to a bunch of guys you probably listen to all week anyway via their sermon podcasts, except that you're paying a premium to do it while sitting at the Yum! Center in Louisville instead of through your headphones. So you're not going for the content.

You're not going for the city either in that it's always either in Louisville or Indianapolis.* **EDITOR'S NOTE:** The Gospel Coalition (TGC) used to be in Chicago and then Orlando, but apparently they realized those cities offered too much fun potential. No offense to those great cities, but I'm not leaving the house to go to Indianapolis in February. **EDITOR'S NOTE:** Ted is also

---

* I used to live in Indianapolis and love it dearly to this day! It's an underrated Midwestern city in that it's impossible to get lost there, you have both the NFL and the NBA, and, all things considered, it has a pretty moderate winter situation.

not leaving his house to go to Indianapolis the other 11 months of the year unless someone offers him tickets to the NFL Combine.

Conferences are church camp for grown men in that you get to hang out a whole bunch, sleep under the same roof, eat a snack that someone else provides, listen to a talk and then talk about all the ways you would have done it better, hear some music, and then go to bed. EDITOR'S NOTE: Women's conferences are strikingly different in that they are usually at nice hotels or resorts and feature some level of pampering. Rinse and repeat. Maybe I just don't understand extroverts who choose to do this and who *want* to run into a bunch of people at the hotel continental breakfast in the morning.

Random conference memories, ranked from worst to best:

- A Campus Crusade conference I went to in Indianapolis in the late '90s in which two bro-ish dudes reenacted a scene from *Braveheart** onstage (because of course). I am the only bro-ish dude on the planet who didn't care for *Braveheart*, and this has always frustrated me.

- An adoption conference at a San Antonio megachurch I spoke at once, which is the first time I truly understood the commodification of adoption as a "thing" and realized my book was about three years too early.

- The Moody Pastors' Conference I wrote about before where I sneaked KK into the dorm—a strangely erotic experience.

- The American Football Coaches Association (AFCA) Coach of the Year Football Clinics I used to go to with my dad and Chuck Shroyer, who was the Al Davis of Hartford City, Indiana, peewee football. We had a blast.

---

* An hour too long and made during Mel Gibson's "I'm never editing out a scene I'm in" phase. Also, I never really bought Mel as an action hero.

The genius of conferences seems to be that it gives you a chance to travel and get away and see your friends, but under the guise of a "work thing" and, even better, a "work thing" that somebody else pays for. In this, it might be the perfect business model, which raises the question, Why are we not hosting a conference?

BP I have thoughts, many thoughts. However, since Ronnie is a professional conference attender and has earned the aforementioned moniker, I feel he should go first. It doesn't help that every one of the hundreds (literally) of conferences I have attended have been for work or as a speaker. So I have observed a lot but never as a willing participant who wanted to be at grown-up summer camp.

RM The conference thing happened for me later in life, to be honest. Of course, I had performed (concerts, a.k.a. music) at conferences on occasion and played at bazillions of festivals, which are the music equiv of conferences (unless you go to an actual "worship" conference, which is just a regular conference where people "talk" about music more than they play it). But my first foray into the world of conferencing was at TGC over a decade ago in Chicago. It's hard to remember what stuck out to me.

So here are seven things:

1. Seeing massive—and I mean massive—amounts of hanging posters of celebrity pastors promoting ESV Bibles.

2. Seeing hundreds of men wearing khakis, blue suit jackets, and multicolored ties like they belonged to some society I didn't know about. Or maybe it was just Ligonier. Which is also a society I happened to know nothing about.

3. Being approached by a kindhearted Canadian pastor in his early fifties ("So I guess old guys like these conferences

too," I said to myself, now the same age as said guy) who ate lunch with me and told me all about his ministry. This was a surprising turn of events, but one that made me think that conferences could be a place to make new friends. Or just listen to pastors tell you all about their ministries, which is also a pastor's most favorite thing in the world to do.

4. Attending with my wife, which was great because it only took us three days before we saw another woman, and it was Mary Kassian, a breakout speaker.

5. Seeing Alistair Begg walking alone through the conference corridors, looking very deep in thought, which he may well have been. Or maybe he was just trying to escape, and I'd actually bet a hefty sum on the latter now that I'm thinking about it.

6. Seeing also a tall, lanky dude in a yellow polo wandering around the same empty corridors (confession: I don't actually know what a corridor is) as people kept pointing and waving at him. I had no idea who it was until years later, when I realized it was Matty Chan. **EDITOR'S NOTE:** It's been fun to watch the fashion arc for Matty Chan over the years. He did the polo shirt as a sort of post-seminary-Baptist-frat-boy thing for a while but moved away from them for a few years. At the time of this writing, however, he's fully embraced the middle-aged-dad look with seasonal polos back in the rotation, but with cowboy boots. Which is only fitting for a former cattle magnate.

7. Being surprised by the scale of it all. There was a ginormous exhibit hall with miles of green-and-purple carpet, megatron jumbo screens, corporate TV crews running all over the place,

and security guards posted at every corner. I remember looking at Big M, thinking, *They're REALLY not trying to be cool here, are they?* And I kind of oddly respected that too.

So there they are. Seven arbitrary recollections that one might think had the potential to make me strangely ambivalent or obviously adverse to ever attending another conf again. But the thing is, I liked it as much as I loathed aspects of it. I liked being in an environment where I could observe people (read: extroverts) doing things that puzzled me on one hand but that were also tied to me on some theological level on the other. It was a new experience. It wasn't so much about the conference talks as it was about talking to people at a conference. With purple carpet. And jumbo screens. And mountains of ESV Bibles.

TK Baby, you've gotta love a Christian conference with larger-than-life-sized posters, screened images of pastors adorning every wall, and NBA-sized crowds and at which a third of the talks are all about the dangers of Christian celebrity. We haven't really lived until we've seen a 50-foot-tall Carl Trueman on the screen telling us not to do the very thing that we're doing.

Don't you think that part of the pathology of being a Reformed guy in a conference setting is that some small part of you has to do the performative thing where you're really enjoying it but you have to publicly eschew the fame part? Baby, that's what I respect about you...there is no ambivalence about wanting conferences and wanting to main-stage with all your heart. I feel oddly comforted by the fact that you're at least being honest about it.

Also, help me understand the business side of this whole deal. Doesn't the Christian publishing industrial complex kind of run the whole conference business? I mean, I probably owe my publishing career to the fact that *Why We're Not Emergent* was given away at T4G (or TGC) many years ago,

at which point all the pastors in that room ran home and blogged about it.*
Short of that happening, the book would have probably sold 3,000 copies and been quickly forgotten. EDITOR'S NOTE: An experience with which all
three of our authors are intimately familiar. Kevin DeYoung (KDY) never
would have gotten famous. I never would have gotten to sneak my wife
past the Moody gestapo before then having furtive, [redacted, redacted,
redacted] dorm room [redacted] with her. Sigh. Maybe I love conferences
too.

BP Ted, if I'm reading this right, and I think I am, what you love is not
conferences. It is royalty money and dorm room [redacted].

I spent almost 15 years in the Christian publishing world, which means
that I was present (I hesitate to say "attended") at literally hundreds of conferences and conventions. My lanyard collection was a thing of beauty. This
also means I saw far more of the exhibit floor, bookstore, and even the occasional greenroom than I did the actual conference meeting or main stage.

For me a conference was like entering a different dimension. The
moment I set foot in the convention center or hotel ballroom, time
ceased to exist. There was a low-grade energy pulsing through everything,
enhanced by the smell of rental carpet and pipe-and-drape setups. Normal rules of human interaction ceased to exist. I made friends who I literally only ever saw at conferences, but in some cases, that meant six times a
year (or three times as much as I saw my parents).

Over the years, there was almost a seasonal consistency with these conferences, knowing what to expect from whom, what to dread, and who you
could guarantee would be there.

---

* On their WordPress blogs in which the banner image across the top was a stack of books
  adjacent to a cup of coffee and were all cleverly named something that had to do with
  books and coffee.

- **TOGETHER FOR THE GOSPEL (T4G):** More accurately known as Together for Calvinism, 10,000+ pastors and seminarians gather together to listen to the same six men preach 60-minute sermons for three straight days. Then they swarm like a plague of locusts to the Zero Dollar Bookstore, where they collect huge stacks of theological resources (like Ted's aforementioned *Why We're Not Emergent*). In between the deluge of books and sermons, the Presbyterians (and some rogue Baptists) find local brew pubs at which they drink stouts and tip badly. The rest of the Baptists drink sweet tea at the Old Spaghetti Factory. And all of them discuss how they would have preached that text differently.

- **THE GOSPEL COALITION (TGC):** Together for the Gospel but chill and with breakouts (including some taught by, gasp, *women*). Per capita, there are fewer blazers and more beers consumed at this conference. And no free books. Attendees live for the glimpse of John Piper, Tim Keller, or Matt Chandler roaming the convention center corridors.

- **THE SOUTHERN BAPTIST CONVENTION ANNUAL MEETING:** The Republican National Convention for pastors combined with the longest church business meeting ever. Lots of hairspray (on pastors and their wives). All beers consumed are surreptitious and not expensed to churches.

- **THE PCA GENERAL ASSEMBLY:** Like the SBC convention but with some renegade Democrats as well as much beer and many cigars, all of which are expensed to churches.

- **THE BETHLEHEM CONFERENCE FOR PASTORS:** Like T4G but much smaller and more relaxed. Also, it's in Minnesota in

February, so every attendee is at least a little crazy. A surprising number of college students in attendance with that crazed, cage-stage Calvinist gleam in their eyes.

- **CATALYST:** Unlike all previously mentioned conferences. And, really, unlike any other conference. Catalyst is a leadership-y, influencer-driven, attractional-church-funded, beautiful-people-platforming, hipster hype machine. They have been known to offer camel rides, have bouncy houses for adults, and do hot-air balloon rides, and all that is before you enter the arena (yes, arena). Each session is kicked off by Hillsong Elevation Passion Bethel Worship in fedoras. And then a string of bestselling inspirational authors recap their books as TED Talks (though, to be fair, most of these books started as TED Talks and should have stayed that way). The best part is that each year, they bring in one token preacher, and let me tell you, John Piper in his faded tweed earnestly extolling the significance of Christ on the cross is quite...dissonant.

- **BASICS CONFERENCE:** See Bethlehem Conference for Pastors but without the college students and overflowing with various accents from the British Isles and more Gettys leading worship.

- **MOODY PASTORS' CONFERENCE:** See Basics Conference but dispensationalist and with all the pastors sleeping in college dorms. They may still be trying to kill the emergent church.

- **THE VERGE CONFERENCE:** A church-planting, urban ministry, multiethnic conference held in a supercool city: Austin. Oozed cool. Loved the TED Talk format with 25 speakers talking for eight minutes each. Attendees and exhibitors alike prioritized this conference for the BBQ.

- **EVANGELICAL THEOLOGICAL SOCIETY:** The fact that this one is called a "society" serves as a good clue as to its nature. The one conference where people are not there to hear speakers but to speak. Or rather to read. To read papers. To read papers about esoteric, incomprehensible theological topics. All while wearing ill-fitting khaki slacks and blue blazers.
- **SUNDRY CHURCH-HOSTED CONFERENCES:** Never meet the attendance projection given to exhibitors to justify the cost. Usually one A-list speaker they blew the majority of their budget on and the rest of the speaking lineup filled out by the church staff. The host church is usually manically eager for the affirmation of exhibitors (but just as ready to ignore them if the A-lister wanders by).

RM I mean, it's an era we're in, is it not? What's funny is that most of the pastor dudes I talk to now who spent half their church budgets on attending these things over the past decade all tell me they're "conferenced out." There's a very peculiar fatigue that comes with attending too many of these big events, which is why so many of us feel drawn to smaller, less flashy conferences. For me, it's become all about people and connections. Here's how some of them play out:

1. That person you were on a ministry staff with back in the day who you bump into at the Crossway table in the middle of the bookstore. For some reason, you're shocked that they're there, even though...umm...*everybody* is there. The problem is, you weren't super tight with them back in the day, so it's hard to remember anything about them. "So...*Gentle and Lowly* is like

the bomb, amirite?" is probably the easiest conversation starter you'll have.

2. That closer friend who's part of the denomination or network you're in, and before you've even said hi, they're asking you when you can get coffee, lunch, dinner, or all three. For the next three days.

3. That social media "friend" that you've never actually met but can somehow pick you out of a crowd, even when they're standing approximately two miles away at the other end of the convention center. This meeting can go either way. You can just as easily receive a vague and confused "Ohhhh...hey..." or an emotionally bonkers faux-reunion-level greeting that rivals a soldier returning home to his family after the Second World War ended.

All said, I'm here for it.

TK I think we're talking about different things here: conferences themselves and fame, which is a by-product of the conferences that are (stay with me) kind of the ultimate fame-flex. And, yes, Pipe, to your question a few pages ago, it is primarily about hotel sex with my wife and book money for me. I am very human.

I think what Ron is talking about is some version of high school but for adults. Substitute "cafeteria" or "Sadie Hawkins Dance" for the energy that Ron described just above, and that's it. And, baby, we *know* you're here for it because we also know you're (literally) not here for the show roughly half the year due to your, ahem, *ambitious* conferencing schedule. Perhaps this is a function of attending tiny, weirdo Christian high schools and not really having the ultrasocial high school experience for real?

I think at a deeper level, it speaks to something that I hear a lot of pastors struggling with, which is the idea that they can't/don't have many (any?) actual friends in their communities with whom they can be real, so they have to seek that kind of kinship/relationship out at a Hampton Inn in Louisville five to six times a year. I'm being glib there, but I actually think that's a real thing and a real problem for which conferences are an imperfect-but-the-best-shot-we-have kind of solution. Thoughts?

Also there's the fame thing. I have a friend who now works at a relatively high level in the Christian leadership industry, and he indicated to me that fame is more a function of "organization" than any kind of individual insider/outsider dynamic that we usually attribute to it (fame). And he explained that main-staging at a conference—Ron's very special dream—is more just a function of being made the "face" of a particular organization. So the main stager is, in a sense, there just as an emissary of whatever organization they are being the smiling face for. Knowing this makes you feel either better or worse about the whole conference thing. Personally, it makes me feel worse. I want to feel like there's something magical or ethereal about fame—something beyond just being (literally and figuratively) platformed by a larger organization.

BP It's fascinating to me that y'all are approaching this topic from such different directions. Ronnie, you're all in, engaging it as a willing but observant participant. Ted, you're observing as an outsider, and a suspicious or even cynical one at that. I think I land somewhere between y'all, something more akin to working the family business. I mean, I've literally been working at conferences since I was ten and I volunteered at the fledgling Bethlehem Conference for Pastors. So I am an insider of sorts. I'm cynical. And part of me still has an insatiable draw to conferences even though I kind of hate them, kind of like the Kennedy kids must feel about politics.

Ronnie, you're absolutely right about conferences becoming more about the people than the platform. There were friends I would see three or four times a year at conferences where we'd grab coffee or stay up late over drinks or get dinner. That's more time than I spend with extended family in a given year. I know guys who have scheduled reunions with former coworkers at various conferences—"Wednesday night is pizza with the old staff, right?" And I'd be remiss if I didn't mention all the awesome interactions we've had with *The Happy Rant* listeners at various conferences over the years. **EDITOR'S NOTE:** This is entirely genuine. It is awesome to meet our listeners live and in the flesh at conferences. You genuinely can maintain meaningful friendships simply through conferences, and that is hands down the best thing about them. (To be fair, the people aspect can get super weird too. Without going into details, let's just say *a lot* of seminarians lack basic social skills.)

Ted, I'm not sure if I can ease your pain or not, but this might help. Your friend's observation about fame applies largely to industry conferences, where *leadership* is the thing. Being the face of a brand or institution carries more weight there. Fame is still pretty ethereal in ministry circles. I mean, *Gentle and Lowly* has sold a bajillion copies, but Dane Ortlund isn't headlining any conferences. Kevin DeYoung headlines a couple conferences, and it would be tough for most pastors to name his last three books. We all still know who Mark Driscoll and James MacDonald are, but they aren't likely to be asked back to speak at *our* conferences anytime soon (though they still get asked elsewhere). Francis Chan is a Christian household name, and nobody even knows what he is doing these days. Eugene Peterson is the pastor everybody is aspiring to be these days, but they didn't decide that until after he passed away. So Christian fame is still a nebulous, undefinable, unpredictable thing.

Let me throw y'all this question: What makes a good conference in your minds?

TK I've identified a core issue with conferences for me: If I go to a conference (or retreat, or trip, or whatever we're calling it), I almost always return with a new acquaintance who invariably ends up feeling really offended if I don't become their new best friend and keep in touch all the time afterward. Conference friendships are, like camp romances/friendships, unsustainable, unless both parties understand exactly what they're dealing with (which is a camp friendship). I run into this dynamic probably one or two times a year, and dealing with the inevitable cycle of unmet expectations/fallout actually occupies a lot of my energy/mindspace.

So for me, it's just easier not to go. For me (again), a conference in which this doesn't happen—or in which I make friends but friends who sort of *innately* understand what is and isn't happening—would be a nice conference.

But nobody really addressed my pastors-not-really-having-real-friends issue from a few paragraphs ago. Is that a thing? Or is that kind of a dead topic? The reason I ask is that I think it kinda goes hand in hand with the please-be-my-new-best-friend thing that I deal with vis-à-vis conferencing. I'm just curious.

RM No, baby, pastors not really having real friends is an issue that's getting talked about quite a lot these days. To be honest, I feel like this could have been it's own chapter. But I would agree that it's probably connected to conferencing because that's the only place ministry dudes are going to find other people who want to talk about Bavinck and debate obscure Augustinian philosophies while drinking adult beverages in a posh downtown hotel pub. **EDITOR'S NOTE:** In a pub because the pastors being described would never lower themselves to drinking in a bar, so they call what is very obviously the hotel bar a pub so they can feel like part of the Inklings or something. The problem is that once the conference is over, most fall back into the plush leather chairs of their introverted pastoral studies and experience the kind of isolation and loneliness that pastoring is known for, and that just got dark, didn't it?

To Pipe's question, a good conference is many things to many people. Here are a few things that make it good for me.

- **Location.** It's going to be a draw for me only if it's in driving range, and by driving range, I mean as close to my front door as possible. Also, large, confusing, metropolitan areas are not ideal because I want to get there, find parking, and not feel like Google Maps is reading a dissertation on the hypostatic union back to me. A smaller city with nice restaurants and neat coffee shops is really all I require.

- **Bookstore.** I enjoy a good bookstore, and not because I'm a huge book lover (I prefer a good album, to be honest) but because I like looking at and buying books even more than I like reading them. If that just made someone on nerd-Twitter gasp, I get it. **EDITOR'S NOTE:** A good bookstore benefits from the conference as well because pastors on a travel budget are like kids in candy stores with birthday money.

- **Speakers.** I like me some good conference speakers, but honestly, I don't go to the sessions like I used to unless I'm with my wife, and then she goes to the session while I meet with a friend. It's a good marriage, guys.

- **Candy.** I love it when the vendors have bowls of candy just sitting on the table, beckoning me into their marketing schemes. "I've always dreamed of going to Bavinck Seminary because you all seem to place a high value on expository preaching, and— oh, I see you have Twix bars. Don't mind if I do…" (Grabs said Twix bar and steps away nervously.)

- **Diversity.** I'm a devoted people watcher, and conferences are super good for that. Nothing like seeing the Spurgeon-loving, 1689-style long-beards kicking it alongside the khakis and blue sport jacket seminarians who look like they just won a PGA tournament. It's deluxe entertainment, I'm telling you.

TK Pipe, I just want to point out that "diversity," in Ron's paradigm here, means having *both* kinds of white guys—beards/tats and PGA types. Do your worst.

BP Ronnie, you forgot another key demographic in the "diverse" conference schema: unkempt college dudes. They inevitably carry large backpacks with multiple things clipped on with carabiners, one of which definitely includes a Nalgene bottle or Klean Kanteen. They don trucker hats and/or bandanas, and their feet are shod with Birkenstocks or Chocos.*

I think what many of these questions come down to is purpose. What is the *purpose* of conferences? The people and ministries putting them on have one set of ideas. They are putting together a stellar lineup of brilliant (by their own estimation) speakers who can collectively expound upon a theme for the spiritual and intellectual benefit of attendees. They see themselves as providing a service and learning opportunity attendees cannot get anywhere else. They may shift the very trajectory of entire churches through their efforts.

The attendees want summer camp with books, beer (even you, Baptists),

---

* Ted here: Pipe, I just want to address your spelling of Chaco. I know this because annually, my wife orders herself a pair, indicating to me that this will be, quote, "a lifetime sandal" and "the only pair I'll ever have to buy." Note that she orders another pair annually.

and candy. The conference is an effective smoke screen so their church members (and especially accountants) can feel good about them going.

And as far as I can tell, it's generally working. Pastors need summer camp and time to hang with friends, but that doesn't sound good to their congregation. But a *conference* with prominent preachers and a Cheesecake Factory–sized menu of breakouts? That they can peddle.

And unlike a mere vacation or bro-trip to a big city, conferences foster deeper conversations and a spiritual environment. Good messages are given that offer encouragement and insight. There's a milieu of genuine meaning in it all. And about once every five or seven years, a conference message is given that becomes a catalyst (pun not intended) in a significant Christian movement.

So I guess what I'm saying is that as weird as conferences are, they're working. They're sort of like lasagna or meat loaf: If you start picking apart the ingredients, they get way less appetizing, but if you leave well enough alone and just dig in, they're not bad at all.

CHURCH HOLIDAY SHENANIGANS

TK I think what's funny about being in Reformed churches most of my adult life is how self-conscious they are about *not* acknowledging any holidays.

It's like, "Hey, I understand that it's Super Bowl Sunday,* but we have that mandatory member's meeting about the budget that we're going to start promptly at 6:30 so that we can make sure that you miss most of the game, because [name redacted] will undoubtedly ask lots of questions and keep us there forever. Also, we could have that meeting at literally any other point in the calendar year, but we're doing it on Super Bowl Sunday to, like, make a point about how spiritual we are and about how little we care about the things of the world."

---

* Yes, to me this is a holiday. I mean, it's way more fun than most allegedly fun holidays, and it's something ecumenical that everyone can enjoy, meaning that it's inclusive, which makes it the best thing in the moral economy of 2021. Also, it provides Ron an opportunity to tweet out some version of "Something about how I'm too cool for / don't understand football...something about what I'm eating...something about my wife" every year. Everybody wins!

Or "Hey, I understand that it's Christmas, but we're just going to go ahead and celebrate the birth of Christ by continuing our verse-by-verse exposition of Leviticus."

That said, I've visited my fair share of other attractional churches with friends and family members over the years, and those are always a blast on holidays, because they go BIG. I went to a megachurch with my mother-in-law on Mother's Day one year, and at one point, the huge theatrical curtains (because "megachurch") peeled back to reveal an IMAX-sized screen on which they showed a film about a mother and her children running together and embracing in a field of wheat. It looked like a Ronnie Martin Christmas card.

I once, surreally, visited a megachurch in the Villages*—that creepy, Shyamalanian planned community in a swamp† north of Orlando—on a Fourth of July, which meant that I got to feel smug and superior about Christian nationalism way before it became trendy‡ to feel smug and superior about that particular topic.

Pipe, I'm guessing your dad didn't do a lot of holiday shenanigans in your church growing up? But, baby, you're Christmas Man, so I'm guessing your church goes big for at least that holiday.

BP There is a different Reformed tradition on holidays: the sanctimonious celebration route. In this tradition, the one I grew up in, all religious

---

* There's probably more here than I can cover in a footnote, but the Villages is known for (a) venereal diseases (which I feel like a 1950s journalist for typing out) and (b) [redacted]. There are also lots of pools, golf courses, and faux-charming town squares, which are supposed to look folksy and old-timey but were actually built a few years ago.

† One of the great real-estate triumphs of all time...getting people to build houses atop swampland that sits two hours away from any beach.

‡ If you're reading this in 2030...(a) bless you and (b) being smug about Christian nationalism became a supertrendy thing during the cultural hellscape that was 2019/2020.

holidays are celebrated in the most overtly churchy way possible. So we didn't celebrate Christmas only; we celebrated Advent. Each Sunday leading up to Christmas involved carols and a "lesson" (which is just a holiday edition of a Bible reading), all while two cherubic children adorned in robes process down the center aisle to light that week's enormous purple wax pillar of a candle. These children carry lances of a sort with open flames at the end and try to light a candle on a pedestal at least two feet taller than they are, so the entertainment value / risk factor was high. Then my dad, the pastor, would read an original epic poem he'd written reflecting on one of the characters of the Bible with an eye toward the coming of Jesus.

On Christmas Eve, we would have a candlelight service at 10:45 p.m. so that as we sleepily walked out, we could wish each other a "merry Christmas" without lying. **EDITOR'S NOTE:** This service lasted an hour and fifteen minutes. In the Reformed tradition, that's usually just the pastoral prayer or call to worship. Those were the only times I ever wore pajamas to church. (Well, other than when I was dragged along to the all-night prayer meetings that kicked off each new year.) I'm pretty sure it was just a ploy to get kids to sleep later than 5 a.m. on Christmas Day.

For other holidays (Maundy Thursday, Good Friday, Thanksgiving), we would gather with other neighborhood churches and do a delightfully awkward ecumenical service that took on the flavor of whatever church was hosting. The female Lutheran minister would read homilies she'd gotten straight from a book. The Evangelical Covenant minister would tell lengthy, aimless stories about his grandpa Sven. The Missionary Baptist Church, a Black church, was the best. Their choir was two men and about seven ladies, and they sang like they were calling heaven down. And their preacher preached like we were about to march into heaven's gates. The services our church hosted were, well, Reformed Baptist.

The Super Bowl and Fourth of July were never even acknowledged by my church. And here's the thing: That made them awesome. I actually sorta hated all the other holidays because they meant endless church services. All my childhood religious holidays were marred by ill-fitting blazers, clip-on ties, postponed meals, the smell of unfamiliar church sanctuaries, and the same tired hymns and carols. But not the Super Bowl or Fourth of July! Those were bastions of gluttony and excess, of explosions and commercial glitz, of real actual fun.

TK The only good thing about any ecumenical service is being able to be smug about doing one. But that's literally it. The ecumenical service is the church-basement potluck of the worship world. There are a ton of options, and they all suck.

Also, there's a *very* small subset of Reformed guy who writes their own epic poetry. I know a few of these guys, and while I have no real desire to hang out with any of them, I'm glad that they exist in the same way that I'm glad there are kids who still think they're going to be an astronaut or the president. It's quaint and ridiculous and cute in much the same way.

RM It's gonna sound crazy given how much of my year is spent thinking, dreaming, and planning for the holidays (and by *holidays*, plural, I mean one holiday—Christmas), but I'm not a super fan of church holiday she-nanigans, on either the plus or the negative side. What I mean is, I grew up in distinctly non-church-calendar evangelical churches where Christmas was neither overblown ("COME SEE OUR NATIVITY WITH LIVE CAMELS AND REAL BABIES THIS SATURDAY NIGHT") nor underplayed ("Since it's Christmas in three days, we thought it would be appropriate to open with 'O Come, O Come Emmanuel' this morning"). My experiences usually consisted of a Christmas tree on stage, a hymn or two leading up to the big day, and a Christmas Eve service that was promoted with all the enthusiasm of a weekly Bible study for seniors. Basically a "Merry Christmas, and God bless us all, everyone" kind of affair.

As a pastor, both extremes drive me a little bonkers, but I think it's the lukewarm receptions to Christmas that probably make me craziest because I don't travel in those circles where it's normal for Santa Claus to fly over the top of the sanctuary and drop MacBook Pros and flat-screen TVs to the congregation. There's this running cliché in ministry circles that pastors secretly hate the Christmas season, even though they're not allowed to say it because that's akin to saying you've rejected Jesus and Christianity. And Easter is a nonstarter, although I'd like to take this opportunity right now to say that Easter is my least favorite holiday "celebration."

Having said that, and if I don't get to say it later, it's been a privilege knowing you boys, and please let me know when you find a new cohost.

But while I'm still here, let me add that it's not that I'm against the resurrection and new life with Jesus as much as I don't enjoy wearing pastel dress shirts from Express, which feels justifiably reasonable to me. **EDITOR'S NOTE:** It's clear Ronnie is not Southern, or this would have read "seersucker suits and bow ties." Although I will say that I do love a good old-fashioned Easter-egg helicopter drop, but that's because I'm a traditionalist.

For real though, I think it's not so much Christmas/Easter itself (obvi) but all the hoopla surrounding it that makes it such a stressful time. So this brings us to some of the beauties of church planting.

The first beauty is that you are not held to any prior traditions, which is the thing that gives way to congregational expectations. In fact, what you get to do as a church planter is create the traditions that the pastor coming after you will have to fight with everyone over, and I promise I take no pleasure in pointing that out but maybe a little.

The other beauty is that I decided from the get-go that holidays would be an enjoyable time for the church instead of a stressful one. That doesn't mean we underplay it. It means we enjoy Christmas to its fullest by not overburdening our people with all kinds of extras. And for some of the extra things we do have to do, like decorate the stage for our live reenactment of Luke chapter 2 complete with giraffes for accuracy, we turn it into a Christmas party. Which for some will feel like a burden, so forget everything I just said.

But that's always the question for me. Not to be too Charlie Brown here, but how do we celebrate Christmas rightly and joyfully without it becoming a big commercial catastrophe? Again, I'm only mentioning Christmas here because those other "holidays" aren't holidays.

TK Baby, I'm really glad you mentioned the pastel Express shirt with tie for Easter. It's one of my least favorite things in the world. Even the candies associated with Easter end up being pastel and, in my opinion, gross.* It's a big milk-chocolate holiday, as opposed to dark chocolate. To me, the whole thing just comes off as treacly and saccharine and fake. If I were Brett McCracken, I'd probably take an additional 2,000 words to make a broader cultural point that I would deftly tie into the milk-chocolate/dark-chocolate thing, but our readers are smart, and I think they can probably get there on their own.

You guys are men of the cloth, so I should probably let you handle the Christmas issue, but to me, I think celebrating Christmas rightly, joyfully, and noncommercially is probably more a matter of the heart than a matter of my church's programming, right? I mean, if I'm viewing Christmas as a chance to joyfully celebrate the birth of Christ with the people I most love, I'm probably doing it right, right?

---

* My wife eats Peeps, which I have no use for and, frankly, have trouble understanding the existence of. It's a tiny fake bird. I love my wife, and this is literally the only food thing we disagree on.

BP As much as Ronnie is Ronnie Kringle, I am probably Ebenezer Piper or Barnabas Scrooge. I kind of hate Christmas (insert proper caveats here about commercial and cultural Christmas versus the actual birth of Jesus Christ). **EDITOR'S NOTE:** Love how Pipe is acting like this is news to all of you. I hate what Christmas has become in terms of a pervasive soundtrack of trash songs covered by every mediocre artist. I hate that Christmas isn't a holiday or even a season anymore. It's a quarter of the year. I hate that it's the obligatory happy time of year, circumstances be damned. The only good sort of Christmas cheer is the kind poured in the eggnog or hazelnut coffee (two beverages that are basically nutmeg phlegm and brewed potpourri if left on their own).

The same is true for Easter, except that America hasn't totally figured out how to make an "Easter season" yet, so it's a little easier to avoid the oppressiveness.

I *do* love celebrating Christmas with my family and my church. The reason is because we do it simply but full of joy in both places. It is unabashedly about Jesus and unashamedly about tearing into presents right before reveling in innumerable delicious calories.

I love celebrating Easter too. The palpable joy of Sunday worship is exceptional. The buoyancy of Spirit is visible among believers. And of course there's the chance to pack the dinner table with friends and family and devour a feast. I'm always here for that.

Holidays get ruined when they get performative. *Put your smiles on, everyone. It's Christmas! Find your bow ties, pastors. It's Easter!* Spending one-fourth of the ministry year (and probably budget) planning a Christmas weekend blowout and then the next one-fourth doing the same for Easter really seems to miss something. The gospel of Jesus Christ is profoundly *anti*performative. It is good news for those who are bad and generally fail. Jesus was born anonymously in an animal stall, grew up in a backwater, died ignominiously, and rose from the dead with no one to witness it. He eschewed fanfare and laid down His glory. And all that humility and low-liness is *why* we can celebrate, but it seems to me it should probably shape how we celebrate Him.

RM I mean, I don't disagree with your hot take on performatism, Pipe. But I would add that a church that "slides" into that shining, smiley, commer-cial sensibility for the holidays is probably doing it on Sundays too. And this is probably the heart of the issue in some ways, isn't it? EDITOR'S NOTE: Despite this being a rhetorical question, we feel it best to close the debate: Yes, this is the issue.

I always open our Christmas Eve services (which are actually on Christ-mas Eve eve) by saying something along the lines of "If you're new here, what you're going to experience tonight is similar to what you'll experience if you join us on a Sunday morning, minus everyone dressed like shepherds and the rhinoceros on stage. Also, here not to perform for you but to par-ticipate with you as we sing and worship the coming Christ." I'm certainly not saying that my church is getting it right here, but I do want there to be a refreshing sense of realism to who we are as a church and a concerted effort to make sure people don't feel like they're being sold something. Because by the time Christmas Eve rolls around, people have had an entire month of being consumers, so let's work hard in attempting to reverse the trend.

TK I feel a little underqualified to comment here, being the only one who isn't a man of the cloth, but it strikes me that church should be the least per-formative place on earth, right? It should, as Pipe explained above, be our one respite from performance and a place where we are reminded that Christ died for sinners who are weak.

That said, to some degree, your parishioners are performing all the time. Ron wrote about it well in the movie chapter, but these are people who by and large are living their lives via their phones, which is nothing if not a performative act. Crafting a response on Twitter, making an Instagram post… these are inherently performative activities that are well documented (by us and others) to do the opposite of making a person feel happy, fulfilled, at ease, or even more "connected" with others, whatever that means. People probably feel as lonely as they've ever felt, which makes this a unique moment for churches to speak into. In fact, church is probably the longest (an hour, an hour and a half, two hours if it's a Reformed church) many people go each week *without* checking their phones or performing on them in some way. In that, it has the potential to be an extremely refreshing place.

I remember in the late '90s and early 2000s, it was really fun to smugly decry "fakeness" and "smiling, shining, performative" church stuff, but all of that strikes me as relative child's play compared to what people are dealing with now vis-à-vis fakeness. We're probably a lot faker on our phones than we ever ran the risk of being at church during a holiday. I mean, the posed, pastel-shirted Easter "family picture" that is choreographed and then posted on Facebook and that doesn't address the fact that there's massive dysfunction in said family is way more fake than anything happening at church, I'm guessing.

Does that mean don't take the picture? I dunno. I tend to be a little all or nothing about this stuff, meaning that if there's massive (or even niggling) dysfunction in my family, it seems a little disingenuous to choreograph and then post a picture whose implication is that everything is going SO WELL. But then again, family pictures used to be a private activity, and hanging them in the "picture hallway" in your house was as "public" as they ever got. Ditto for senior pictures, vacation pictures, workout pictures, birthday party pictures, I'm-writing-at-my-desk pictures, posed Olan Mills pictures, and so on. None of this used to be for public consumption. Almost everything today strikes me as extremely fake.

I think a person's built-in fake detector is actually proof that we're created in God's image. We *do* hunger for something real, whether it's Christmas, Easter, or a random Sunday in July. So, pastors, be as nonfake on social media as you endeavor to be from the pulpit, and be as nonfake during the Christmas season as you are in July. People will appreciate it.

To quote Bob Sugar in *Jerry Maguire,* "There it is, I said my piece...talk to Rick."

BP I'm with you about everything you just said, Ted. I think where I am still a bit tied up is this: When everything is performative and turned into a big deal, how do we celebrate the actual big deals (you know, like the incarnation or the resurrection of the Son of God)? The answer isn't—it can't be for all the reasons we've written—to outperform or outshindig the world. That actually seems to diminish the significance of Jesus.

I think that means the answer has to be in the spirit of how we celebrate. Nonfake is a good starting point. Heartfelt gratitude and praise. Welcoming the "least of these," not just the beautiful and powerful people. What this adds up to is that we celebrate like we need Jesus rather than like He needs us. We need to celebrate like we aren't trying to impress Jesus (or anyone else) but like we want to introduce people to all the reasons we're excited about Him. This doesn't preclude excellence, but it eliminates the madhouse rat race of showmanship.

It also eliminates the bedraggled, killjoy manner some Christians bring to holidays. Jesus doesn't find us any holier because our faces are dour and our wallets are closed on Christmas. Asceticism and skepticism about happiness are just as performative as gluttony and avarice, except they're not even fun.

I'm also feeling a tad convicted about the performatism of being judgmental about how *others* celebrate. For guys like me, the easiest thing to do might be to sit back and sneer a little at the lavish (or monkish) manner in which others do things. Crapping on others' missteps still smells like crap, after all.

It seems to me that the quickest way to deflate a holiday—or any celebration—is to get tied up in the "proper way" to do it. When we go down that road, we aren't celebrating anymore. We're trying to meet expectations. Instead, I think we should remember Ecclesiastes 9:7: "Go, eat your bread with joy, and drink your wine with a merry heart, for God has already approved what you do." We have freedom to party and worship before God, and if we do it with a merry heart aimed at Him, it's all good.

MANLY MEN

TK I work at a university, and as such it fills me with fear to even type the word "man" in a 2021 context. To some, even the word is aggressive and antiquated. I find that it kind of runs by department. For example, if you're a business administration major who happens to be a man, it's totally okay to walk a certain way and be certain in a certain way and basically act like (stay with me)...a man. If you're an English or social work major, this is off the table for you. It's a tough, confusing deal for those kids. There really should be a pamphlet.*

This one is tough for me because I don't consider myself a razor-blade-gargling, chainsaw-juggling, fire-breathing man† of the sort that is trotted out on a certain kind of stage at a certain kind of conference. Nor do I consider myself the sort of fey, arty, demure, "kinda kinda kinda," effete

---

* Instead, there is Twitter.

† For an archetype of this kind of guy, see early 2000s Mark Driscoll.

intellectual* that is currently all the rage in liberal arts settings all over the country. I'm not a deconstructionist. I'm not a male feminist. I believe things and feel a certain way about things (but not all things) and try not to walk down a hallway like I'm trying to disappear. Nor do I try to walk down the hallway like I want to kill everyone in it. It's a fine line.

I've played and coached football all my life, and I like the kinds of qualities it can impart to players, though I fully assent to the fact that those qualities can come in other contexts—however, they are all contexts that require a certain amount of hard work and sacrifice and the risk of failure. Minus the hard work, sacrifice, and risk, I think it's safe to say that a person won't have those qualities.

I'm trying to raise two young men. I don't especially care if they play football at a high level, or box, or do anything that I used to be passionate about doing. But I *do* care that they learn how to work hard, sacrifice for others, take calculated risks, and confess their sins with regularity. I care that they love their family and love the local church. I think all these things are quantifiably manly, whether the man doing them likes eating razor blades or salad. Or looks a certain way or doesn't.

The thing is, I didn't hate the early 2000s Driscy,† "be-a-real-man" thing because it probably needed to be said at that point, even though it would go over like a lead balloon in 2021 and was probably actually dumb then. **EDITOR'S NOTE:** Ted was not alone; thousands upon thousands of Christian men didn't hate the early 2000s Driscy. He was compelling and touched a nerve and felt like he was filling a void. It's dumb now too because we've (again) reduced manhood to a starter-kit-worthy set of

---

* For an archetype of this kind of guy, see early 2000s Rob Bell, current Rob Bell, the Todd Louiso character in *High Fidelity,* or maybe half the college dudes in your church.

† This take, which I wrote like three weeks ago, has already aged poorly because Driscy is back in hot water for a bunch more stuff.

purchases (flannel, boots, beard, beers) that don't necessarily make any-one quantifiably "manly." And yet there's this pressure to make sure people know we're men, but not exactly-like-Douglas-Wilson-or-insert-another-overly-macho-man men. For example, I feel like we now spend a third of our time on the program making sure people know we think Chainsaw Con 2021 is stupid or that we're too cool/intellectual/nuanced for Douglas Wilson types.

It's confusing and exhausting, and I hate the whole thing, to be honest.

Also, Pipe, I almost wrote a series of books on manhood for Moody Publishers back when my star was rising with them for an editor who wouldn't have "gotten" them and at a time when I didn't even "get" it. It would have been disastrous, and I'm glad it didn't happen.

BP I feel a little on edge right now because I'm at a solid three-fourths on that starter kit. I just can't grow a beard. I do, however, carry a pocketknife pretty much always. So maybe I'm a cliché?

I feel like all the manhood hullabaloo in the last couple decades has lost track of two very important facets of being a man. In fact, these are really the two defining facets: anatomy and following Jesus. I feel a little queasy writing this because it sounds so simplistic and because gender fluidity is the current societal drug of choice. But I just can't escape Genesis 1, where God created man in His image, male and female He created them. And I also can't ignore that Jesus was fully God and fully man and that He was the quintessential man. So God created approximately half the human popu-lation as men *on purpose*, and He meant it as a good thing.

I know this is super basic, almost stupid basic. But when men begin to cower away from being men (and by this, I mean genetically male follow-ers of Jesus) because of our confused, genderless morass of a milieu, I think we need the basics. The same goes for the raw-meat-gnawing-hear-me-roar-women-are-the-weaker-sex-and-emotions-are-weakness faux men too. Lit majors and pipe fitters alike need the basics: God made us this way, and now let's follow Jesus.

I guess my question—and I'm going to try not to caveat this to death—is, How can men take pride in being men without being the jackwagon version of men? What does it look like to live up to what God made us to be? And also, what did He make us to be?

TK Well, per the current social orthodoxy, we can't take pride in being men. But I love what you said there about what God did vis-à-vis creating men. It's not like He's rethinking it. Your question is so hard because there are so many people (ourselves included, at times) taking so much pride in the wrong things.

I'll put it in the context of parenting, which is, if nothing else, an exercise in trying *not* to take pride in the wrong things all the time. Both of our boys have significant gifts, but they both, like all kids, have really significant challenges and shortcomings. So it seems like we're always working back around to statements like "If they love the Lord with all their hearts, take care of their families, and love and serve their churches joyfully, then they're living a good life." All the externals—everything from career choice to income to sports participation to grade point average to beard length—matter very little in light of those other things.

I would prefer they be humble. I'd prefer they not be preening egomaniacs. I would prefer they be the kind of men whose wives and children feel safe while walking down the street with them at night. But the guy that I just described can look a lot of different ways, if that makes sense. They don't have to bench press Buicks or chew glass to be that kind of "man."

RM No, baby, I'm pretty sure chewing glass needs to be part of a quality manhood card until we enter glory and are able to finally swallow those mouthfuls of glass. You're making me *real* afraid with all this "children feeling safe" feminization talk. Is this the part where I need to assure everyone that I'm joking?

TK Honestly (and maybe it's the "academia" talking), I wouldn't have known if you were joking or being serious until you said you were joking. Sigh. **EDITOR'S NOTE:** I can't tell if you're joking about not knowing if I was joking. And Pipe, I don't think you're a cliché for carrying a pocketknife all the time. I do the same thing, primarily because I think knives are cool and it's fun to buy them—making me not unlike most 12-year-old boys. So maybe I'm not a man? I only ever use the knife to open eBay packages. **EDITOR'S NOTE:** Knives work equally as well on Amazon packages and as an adult fidget spinner.

RM Pocketknives? Really, boys? Anyway…I think we're describing a real thing here, especially given the fallout we're seeing from toxic masculinity, which so many have been affected by. But I'm with you, Big T. I think humility is the Christlike cure for men whose tendency is to dominate, which undoubtedly stems from a personal experience they encountered in life. I'm thinking about my own dad here, who definitely came from the school where men fulfilled the traditional roles we think of men doing, and women did the same. I was certainly introduced to some unhealthy behaviors for sure but also some character traits that might have characterized godly manhood as well.

On a personal level, I've always been resistant to machismo, which everyone but a machismo would probably admit to as well, but we are seeing an evangelical subculture that equates manhood with aggression, which

I think we'd all agree is not a page we read in Scripture, *even if* Jesus would have overturned tables every day after lunch during His earthly ministry.

TK Kudos to us for getting to page three of this thing before "toxic masculinity" was written (and unironically). Semiseriously though, it seems like toxic masculinity can be real (like abuses of power and all that), though oftentimes it just stands in for "any man with whom I don't completely agree." That worries me as, you know, a man. Tongue kind of in cheek here, but as I wrote before, a man's only options are to be gay, British, or Jimmy Fallon so as not to be seen as "toxic."

So to play a little devil's (or man's) advocate here: What's the Christlike cure for men whose tendency is to do the opposite of dominate? Whose tendency is to, like, be *demure* to a fault? Because honestly, I don't see a lot of "dominant" types walking around anymore.

RM Baby, I think you've singled out a huge issue, which is not advocating for the devil at all, by the way, because he's a big fan of demurring, which I'm also guessing is a small town somewhere in South Dakota. Demure is a nicer, more *Downton Abbey* version of what we might call passivity, if I'm hearing you correctly. And passivity is a thing, man, because it still seeks to gain control but does it passively rather than forcefully.

TK Baby, that's *big*. I buy it! Continue!

RM What I mean is, passive people seek to retain control by making sure their environment remains stable and unaffected. For a passive person, "not dealing" is how they "deal" with change or upheaval that can create potential discomfort. Of course, this is where the sin of omission can come into play in that the passive person will fail to do what they ought to do. Of course, all of us have areas that we are passive in, even if we can't be described as passive by nature. But I wonder if passivity is the new dominance, if you will.

Social media has made it so that we can express varying levels of dominance but not have to face much of the social repercussions that come with our F&B (flesh and blood) relationships. If this is true, then passivity in our F&L circles becomes our de facto posture, and one that is much easier to manage, if we're being honest. I do know this: Passivity in church culture is a thing that needs to be reckoned with. Obviously, we've learned that it should be reckoned with more gently and lowly than, shall I say, more dominant leaders in the past have dealt with it, but it doesn't make it any less of a problem. Also, I don't think it's anything new. When you read the Gospels, Jesus had to deal with overly passive and nonpassive dudes. It just seems more exaggerated now for some reason.

BP I'm in on that too. I totally buy the idea of passivity being a manipulation ploy. Instead of a "my way or the highway" mentality, it's a "my way or whatevs…I mean, it's fine, really" mentality. And then hurt feelings and seeking pity, which means victimhood. Ergo, control. It's all so predictable though. The passive men are the pendulum-swing generation moving *all* the way away from our fathers' fathers' generation's way of doing it. But without any real heart change.

I grew up under the fathering of the man who cowrote *the book* on roles of men and women—or complementarianism, if we're still allowed to say that. You would think, by stereotype, that he would be an aggressive, emotionally fragile and guarded, brash husk of a man. And you would be wrong if you thought this. He is both a gentleman and a gentle man. He writes poetry to my mom. He is quiet and reserved and careful with his words, especially in social contexts. His complementarianism is based on theological convictions drawn from biblical study, not fragility or insecurity or machismo.

I, on the other hand, am more prone to be brash and loud and confrontational. And I was even more so when I was younger. So I took my father's theological convictions and twisted them to fit my arrogant brashness through my teens and twenties. Which is to say, I was a chauvinistic jerk. I lacked conviction (and had done little biblical study) and functioned by insecurity, familiarity, and convenience.

By God's grace, my own failures, and some strong correction from others, I came to realize my sinfulness and general jerkery. And then the pendulum swung. I resented my dad's position. I wasn't a male feminist (if one can really be such a thing), but I still lacked conviction. So I became passive and tried to control people, particularly my wife, that way.

So, yeah, I see the passivity-as-control thing as an overreaction to dominance-as-control. Except it's probably more insidious because it's so much less obvious.

TK Yeah, I think passivity-as-control is more insidious because it's couched in a sort of goodness that the "user" has probably even convinced himself of on the front end. At least with dominance-as-control, you knew exactly what you were dealing with.

Pipe, I appreciate your transparency there—especially the part about the temptation to use passivity-as-control. I've definitely been guilty of this too...for me in the area of taking an "I'm cool with whatever" posture as a means of getting people to like me.

Real quick, I want to do a paragraph or two in defense of John Wayne, because equating John Wayne (an actor, famous for portraying a certain kind of man) with everything evil and horrible and toxic about being male has become the de rigueur thing to do for a certain kind of Christian...so much so that there are now books* out about it. One, I don't think there

---

* Sigh.

are actually a lot of Christian men taking their cultural cues from an actor whose last movie was released in 1976. Two, though it would be easy to paint John Wayne as a very one-dimensional kind of glass chewer, I also feel like his library* just as often delivers characters with a glass-chewer-with-a-heart-of-gold-type arc. To wit, if Wayne's Rooster Cogburn character— being the kind of character who would defend the life of a 14-year-old girl, lower himself into a snake pit to save the life of said girl, and then ride to the brink of exhaustion and death himself to save her life, after which he declines all forms of payment and simply rides off into the sunset, refusing all book deals, blog tours, podcast appearances, and main stagers in the aftermath—is a terrible person, then sign me up for being a similar kind of terrible person.

Anyway.

Can I ask you a bit of a personal question, since you're raising daughters, and I'm raising boys who (Lord willing) will one day date and maybe even marry Christian women? As a father, what are you looking for out of a potential spouse for your daughters, vis-à-vis this dicey issue? I mean, on the raising boys side, I'm trying to get them to have enough backbone to have actual convictions about things that matter—which goes hand in hand with helping them triage *which* things actually matter as a means of keeping them from being the insufferable guy who feels like he has to die on *every* hill. On the other hand, I'm trying to get them to equally value a humble, repentant spirit and a heart that follows hard after Jesus as the "manliest" thing. I guess that's a complicated way of saying that I want them to lead in a gentle and kind way, but I still want them to lead.

But I wonder if there are things I'm missing. Also, for the record, I'm not trying to do the super-Reformed thing of arranging a marriage between

---

* Which I would call my knowledge of "cursory" at best.

my boys and your daughters, and it pains me to say that this is less of a joke and more of a real thing in some circles.

BP Thank you for clarifying the arranged-marriage thing. I think I lack the requisite livestock to provide a proper dowry.

As to the John Wayne / Rooster Cogburn thing, I generally agree. I recently rewatched *Band of Brothers*, the greatest miniseries ever made, and it had me thinking along the same lines. Were those young men of the "greatest generation" emotionally stunted, unexpressive, insensitive meatheads? I guess, in a sense, if you're comparing them to the clowns from *New Girl*, *Big Bang Theory*, or whatever the latest show rife with aimless, uncommitted, oversensitive, oversexed, immature, grown-up boys is. At least the boys of Easy Company lived for something, gave their lives for their country and for their wives, and were willing to cry about how much they loved each other 50 years later. Sure, they lacked the vocabulary to express deep feelings and affection, but they sure gave every ounce of life for both. We seem to have gone the other way now, where young men are armed with arsenals of words but lack direction, purpose, and passion for things that matter.

Off the top of my head, here are things I would like to see in a young man interested in marrying my daughters:

Personal responsibility: Does he handle his business, own his mistakes, show up on time (or communicate clearly if he can't), and work hard (not to be confused with earning a lot of money or having professional prospects)? I'm less interested in him being "breadwinner" than being the kind of guy who does what needs doing to care for himself and others.

Integrity: I suppose this could be called character. Is he an honest person? Is he willing to fess up to failures? Does he present himself with transparency instead of making himself look better than he is? Does he have friends with whom he is honest, not just golf or work or beer buddies whose average maturity is about 15.5?

Spiritual direction: I'm not expecting my daughters to marry Charles Spurgeon. I would like them to marry someone who is committed to spiritual growth and takes the church, as in a genuine local church, seriously. I think those two things compose a huge amount of what people mean when they say "spiritual leadership" (a complementarian buzzword). I don't need him to "pastor his home." (In fact, if he is keen on "pastoring his home" I would strongly suggest she go looking for Dougy Fresh books in his library and Joe Rogan podcasts on his phone. Then I'd suggest she dump him.) But I very much care if he follows Jesus and takes God's Word seriously.

Kindness: I really hope my daughters marry people who will treat them as equals and who enjoy their company. This takes a lot of faces, but I really want them to feel respected by and have fun with their spouses. Does he listen and take an interest in her? Does he notice when she needs encouragement (or at least try to learn how to notice, since this doesn't come easy for many of us)? Does he know how to have a real conversation where he shares ideas and observations and feelings and also listens to and responds appropriately to hers?

Selflessness: I expect few young men to have this, so the question is whether he shows signs of growing into it. If he has integrity and spiritual direction, he's likely on the right track. I think this and kindness are neck and neck for the most underemphasized traits of a good husband among many complementarians. They want to raise young men willing to lead and die for their families but not sacrifice and live for them. I just don't see how anyone can be a good husband or father without selflessness.

I don't know if this answers your question, Ted. I just really hate the checklist way of writing out what someone should be looking for in a spouse. "Well, he checked 16/20 on my list. I can probably fix another 2, so I guess he'll do." I'm mainly looking for character and spiritual trajectory. The rest will take care of itself. I think leadership is learned and earned more than claimed, so if a young man has character and is growing in the right ways, he can grow into a leader. Really, how many men are great spiritual leaders in the home at 22 or 26? I wasn't.

THE HAPPY RANT DICTIONARY

@JARED C: Jared C. Wilson, who is Ronnie's best friend. Jared lives in Kansas City and has released two new books in the time it took me to type this sentence. He loves Tom Brady, putting out books, and shopping at Marshalls. Being friends with Big R makes him feel cooler, and being friends with Jared makes Big R feel more academic.

BABY: An actual baby, meaning a tiny, pink, sometimes-gross human—also things that Reformed families produce in droves. It's also how I (Big T) refer to Ron (and how he refers to me) due to our shared love of the movie *Swingers,* which came out in the 1990s and starred Jon Favreau and Vince Vaughn—both prefame.

BIG M: Big R's (see below) wife.

BIG R: Ted's nickname for Ronnie Martin.

BIG T: Ron's nickname for Ted Kluck.

CASHISH (CASH-EESH) OR CASHISHE (CASH-EESH-AY): Money. Paper. Whip-out. Bank. Green. Benjamins. Also the thing that all three of us wish we had more of and aren't great at making or managing.

CHANNY (CHAN-EE): Francis Chan (see also Franky Chan). Also Matt Chandler. Channy can stand in for Franky Chan or Matt Chandler.

CHRISTIAN SLUMLORDS: Everybody in Big T's church. This refers to the sudden boom in all Christians wanting to become realtors or own rental properties as a means of getting rich but also, somehow, doing it for Jesus.

CONF: Short for "conference," which (any conference) is the dream destination for Big R, who is all about getting that lanyard, booking that Spirit Airlines flight, and getting out of town for a few days.

DISPY (DISP-EE): Short for "dispensationalist," which was the thing that everybody was before Martin Luther started the Protestant Reformation with Kevin DeYoung in 2006. Dispys love the end-times, rapture novels, Jack Van Impe, and *Thief in the Night.* They sometimes have an affinity for Israel and [redacted] too.

DOUGIE FRESH: Not to be confused with the American rapper from the 1980s. When the boys say Dougie Fresh, it is in reference to Douglas Wilson, who is a famous pastor from someplace out west who likes lighting things on fire both literally and metaphorically. He is either brilliant or a horrible monster depending on who you ask. Ron and Pipe need to put distance between themselves and Dougie Fresh (and do so, verbally, on the regular), while Big T doesn't have a dog* in the Dougie Fresh fight at all. If he did, Dougie Fresh might light said dog on fire.

---

* Literal or metaphorical.

DRISCY (DRISK-EE): Mark Driscoll, who was a metal-necklace-and-Tapout-shirt-wearing pastor in the early 2000s and who is now a guy who lives in Scottsdale and sort of embodies the Scottsdale ethos perfectly vis-à-vis tanning and fashion. He morphed from angry uncle pastor to smug father figure pastor. Trivia: Did you know that Driscy's church was the third one profiled in Collin Hansen's *Young, Restless, Reformed* book? Wild.

DRISCY BUSINESS (DRISK-EE-BUSINESS): Business dealings and news involving Mark Driscoll.

EP: An episode of our podcast—that is, podcasting magic.

FURTY (FUR-TEE): Stephen Furtick*. A megachurch pastor who is at this very moment probably bench pressing a Nissan or overusing Axe body spray. The asterisk connotes probable performance-enhancing drug usage on his part.

HARBOR NETWORK: A rebrand of the Sojourn Network, which is Ron's church-planting network, which is famous for flannel shirts, work boots in which no actual work is done, and lavish conferences. Harbor has nautical/oceanic connotations despite being headquartered in Louisville. Also sounds like a Christian radio network from the late '80s.

JUDAS H. PRIEST: A thing that Ted says when he gets really upset about something. Judas Priest was a metal band in the 1980s featuring Rob Halford's distinctly falsetto voice. It's also just a fun thing to say. Try it.

KK: Kristin Kluck, Big T's wife.

KDY: Kevin DeYoung. The author/pastor who rode Big T's coattails into publishing and who since then may or may not have done a little bit better than Big T, depending on how you look at it (by which I mean literally *all* ways of looking at it). Known also for fecundity.

MAIN-STAGING: The act of headlining a conference, which is a thing that none of the boys have ever done but is aspirational, especially for Big R.

METAXY: Eric Metaxas, who is an author that everybody liked (Bonhoeffer book) and who now everybody hates.

MONEY, THE: This is the ultimate compliment in Big T and Big R's world and, again, is an homage to (or a direct rip-off of) *Swingers*. So, for example, you might say something like, "Baby, your little tiny bespoke leather headphone case is *the money*."

NAPLES, FLORIDA: Ron's dream destination for a little while. Naples is home to lots of rich old people and also humidity. But not (yet) Big R or Big M, much to their chagrin.

NERD TWITTER: Where guys from a certain theological subset gather to let each other know what white papers they're reading and to occasionally drop in a reference to Hebrew. The tweets have no entertainment value per se and are intended only to serve the persona of the person doing the tweeting (which also describes, to be fair, all of Twitter).

PIPE: Our nickname / term of endearment for Piper. What can we say, we like shortening things.

PIPE'S DAD (A.K.A. JOHNNY P): John Piper, who is also an author.

RETREAT: Another of Big R's dream destinations. Kind of like a conference (plane ticket, lanyard) but without the sessions to skip. Very Instagramable.

ROBES: Long, flowing, colorful vestments that Anglicans wear proudly and smugly. Or a friend with a certain kind of car.

RONNIE TARMAC: Ted's nickname for Ron because of Ron's penchant for traveling all the time. The mental image here is one of Ron running out onto an airport tarmac pulling one of those rolling bags.

SLICKY: This is Big T and Big R's term of endearment for a guy named Clinton Faupel, who ran a studio of some kind in Fort Wayne, Indiana. It was either radio or television. Or neither. We got to "Slicky" due to his name being Clinton and due to former President Bill Clinton being referred to as Slick Willie. Stay with us.

SUSS OUT: To elaborate or explain but with flair; an invitation to expound upon an idea and say what you were really hoping to say but wanted to be asked. (Big T might say to Big R "Baby, suss that out" after Big R offers a typically truncated opinion.)

TGC: See below.

T4G: See above.

THE REFORMATORY: A show that Big R and Big T used to host in Fort Wayne, Indiana, which is the Manhattan of East Central Indiana. The show was either radio or television, but nobody really knows. The boys brought lots of wardrobe changes, which was sort of moot due to the low light (pitch dark?) in the studio where they recorded. These trips included lots of movie theater experiences and Zesto ice cream. See also "Slicky."

TIMMY K: A term of endearment the boys use to describe the prolific author/pastor Tim Keller.

TO AND FAR: Trogges's (see below) butchering of the phrase immediately below.

TO AND FRO: Where we wander at the end of every ep.

TOLEDES: Toledo, Ohio, where Ron and Big T once spent a magical writing retreat that included free tickets to a Toledo Mud Hens baseball game and a very forgettable cup of tortilla soup, which was actually just standard tomato soup with avocado slices floating on top. And by "writing retreat," we mean spending 20 minutes at a Panera Bread saying "Looks good" while pretending to look at each other's chapters.

TROGGES (TROW-GS):   Stephen Altrogge, who for about a year and a half was the original host of the *Happy Rant* and who can now help you maximize your earning potential as a marketing content writer working from home. Trogges also wrote "Behold Our God," which is one of the great worship songs of our era.

WHEN BELIEVERS DON'T BELIEVE: The bestselling title of Ted and Ron's very tepidly selling title, *Finding God in the Dark.*

WOLGS: Our literary agent, Andrew Wolgemuth, who has made several thousands of dollars by partnering with us over the years and who will make hundreds on this particular book.

YODA (YO-DUH): Yoda was a character in a popular movie franchise called *Star Wars* but is now a term for a certain style of tweeting in which the writer tries to be equal parts profound, opaque, and (choose one) woke/sensitive/inspirational. The world's greatest Yoda tweeter is Timothy Keller, who got great at it without even trying. Ron is currently trying to make headway in the Yoda Twitter game.

APPENDIX A
MOVIE RUSHMORES

BY TED KLUCK

The conceit here is pretty simple—I (Ted) am choosing my movie "Rushmores" (four movies or movie-related things) in each category. I don't know who first invented this conceit, but it was probably Bill Simmons.

SPORTS MOVIE RUSHMORE

Hoosiers: First of all, you've got small-town Indiana in the fall, the 1950s, letterman jackets, and high school basketball. Add to that an incredible cast (Gene Hackman, Barbara Hershey, Dennis Hopper) and some real brokenness/redemption/reconciliation, and you have maybe the perfect movie. Also a sneaky-great soundtrack that may or may not cause me to weep silently each time I listen to it. This movie is also on my "shots of corn-fields and silos in movies" Rushmore and my "guys taking girls for a romantic walk around the edge of a cornfield" Rushmore.

Moneyball: Aaron Sorkin was involved in this, so you knew the script was going to be good. There is an astonishing number of alpha males in this movie, including Brad Pitt's Billy Beane character and the late, great Philip Seymour Hoffman's Art Howe character—both of whom, in their own ways, pull off the "menacing, swaggering ex-athlete" thing really well. Mix in just enough baseball,[*] just enough math, and just enough family stuff,[†] and you have a sports movie without a clichéd ending that is pathologically rewatchable.

Field of Dreams: "No, Ray, it was you." This would make my "movies set in the Midwest" Rushmore too (as would *Hoosiers*) and is great because it glorifies corn, Iowa, writing, and baseball. The city of Boston also gets a great ten-minute run in this movie, which has father-son stuff, baseball stuff, existential middle-aged guy stuff, and Ray Liotta minus the cocaine and despair (this is a reference to *Goodfellas*). It's like they made a movie just for me.

Friday Night Lights: It's sad to me that people know the *FNL* narrative more from the television show than from this movie or the tremendous book that it's based on. This movie caused me to buy up all available shares of Garrett Hedlund stock because I thought he would be Hollywood's next hot, charismatic leading-man-of-a-certain-age.[‡] This obviously didn't happen. However, this is an amazing movie set in 1988 with an incredible 1988 soundtrack (lots of Poison and Public Enemy) that both glorifies and casts a

---

[*] "Hatty, grab your bat...you're hitting for Burnsie."

[†] The scene with Spike Jonze dating Billy's ex-wife is gold...the one where Jonze's character is so clearly overwhelmed by the magnitude of Billy's alphaness that he can barely get out a sentence. Also Billy's wife is the actress from *The Princess Bride*.

[‡] Unfortunately, the market was flooded with the Ryans (Reynolds and Gosling) and Hemsworths (Chris and Liam). I still have a few shares of Hedlund, though.

critical glance at high school football—both of which are appropriate ways to approach the topic.*

Honorable mention: *Any Given Sunday:* Actually, this movie was terrible, but Ron and I just wanted to write about it (does move). This is Oliver Stone's bloated, over-the-top paean to professional football† starring Al Pacino doing an impression of Al Pacino‡ circa *Scent of a Woman.* This movie is an hour too long and tries to juggle one too many story lines. If you make it 33 percent less ridiculous and remove either the Shark Lavay§ or Cameron Diaz story lines...you have a real movie. Also, Aaron Eckhart is *completely* believable as the Kyle Shanahan figure in this one...the ahead-of-his-time genius play caller.

BRAD PITT RUSHMORE

Inglourious Basterds: Brad plays Lieutenant Aldo "The Apache" Raine in this one—a Nazi-hunting, wildly charismatic stud with a Midwestern/Southern drawl that makes him sound equal parts super menacing and super down to earth. This is Quentin Tarantino, so all the caveats vis-à-vis horrific over-the-top violence¶ apply here, but this film has an amazing Brad performance offset by a whole bunch of other actors doing their finest work and an outstanding script.

---

* If you're wondering where *Rocky* is (and who could blame you?), it's because it gets a whole category below.

† Trivia: This movie launched Under Armour as a brand.

‡ However, if you were to play Pacino's "Die for That Inch" speech for me right now, I would hang on to every word, probably rewind/rewatch, and maybe get misty-eyed over it.

§ This hurts due to my love for Lawrence Taylor.

¶ A whole rash of Nazis get shot, stabbed, scalped, and blown up in this movie.

Once upon a Time in Hollywood: This movie also makes my "movies about friendships between dudes" Rushmore because it's tangentially about a re-imagining of the Manson murders in Hollywood but is more about putting Brad and the equally charismatic Leonardo DiCaprio on-screen together in as many scenes as is humanly possible in one movie. If you love the late 1960s and early 1970s, you'll love the songs, cars, T-shirts, set designs, fashion, and also every other thing about this movie.

The *Ocean's* franchise: Brad eating. Brad wearing shiny shirts. Brad pulling off heists with his wildly charismatic buddies. Brad playing poker. Brad watching television. Brad in Vegas, Amsterdam, and then Vegas again. I'm in. Also, Elliot Gould.

Legends of the Fall: This is peak early career Brad at his long-haired, charismatic, girl-stealing best, in an epic, sweeping, World War I–era family drama that portrays brokenness and sin for the life-crushing hell-bound race that it actually is, with a tiny (and super satisfying) crackle of redemption at the end.

ROMANTIC COMEDY RUSHMORE

You've Got Mail: No one has ever looked cuter in a movie than Meg Ryan circa this movie. Also my favorite kind of Tom Hanks movie and my favorite kind of New York movie. Also glorifies writing and the book business. My wife always says (a little too gleefully) that I remind her of the Frank Navasky character.

Notting Hill: This movie features London, a small bookstore, and Hugh Grant being charming. I'm in.

Love Actually: This movie features London, Christmas, and Hugh Grant being charming as the prime minister. It also features Bill Nighy doing Bill

Nighy things, which in this case means being a loveable old rascal who is also a rock star.

Jerry Maguire: This is also a "sports movie" Rushmore* candidate and is also maybe a drama with comedic moments. Also it's the perfect midcareer-Tom-Cruise movie in that he started playing thoughtful, flawed characters, and really well. This, to me, is the best kind of Cruise role...I wish he would do more of these.

Honorable mention: *Elizabethtown:* This is a Cameron Crowe movie that critics mostly hated but I love in that it deals with father-son stuff, family stuff, achievement stuff, sneakers, and a girl making an epic mixtape for a guy. It's also the only movie in which I've ever really liked Orlando Bloom.

COSTUME DRAMAS SET IN ENGLAND RUSHMORE

Downton Abbey: This is a series that was made into a movie, but I'm handling the whole *Downton Abs* universe in this section. This series is a shining example of the kind of slow-burn storytelling that used to be a thing but really isn't anymore, what with the proliferation of Marvel-type moviemaking. If you like manners, restraint, elaborate-plated dinners, tuxedos, and characters changing over a multitude of years and scenarios...you'll love this.

Pride and Prejudice (the BBC version with Colin Firth): I'm a little bit of a snob about this one, but this is the only version of *Pride and Prej* that I personally ride with. Firth is amazing as the sometimes-awkward, sometimes-obnoxious Darcy[†], and Jennifer Ehle is as close to the Elizabeth Bennet

---

* Also joins Alan Alda's *Paper Lion* on the "movies about the St. Louis / Phoenix / Arizona Cardinals" Rushmore.

† I also have a take about this wherein in you replace any Mr. Darcy in any adaptation with Tom Hardy, and the movie becomes like 33 percent better, immediately. Think about it. He's handsome, he's amazing at brooding. There's no downside.

from the book as you're gonna get on-screen. She's amazing and should have been a way bigger movie star.

Gosford Park: This is a fun murder mystery, kind of along the lines of *Clue* meets *Downton Abbey.* It's rich people in an English mansion, featuring Jeremy Northam and Bob Balaban. I'm here for any and all Balaban content.

Emma (the one with Jeremy Northam and Gwyneth Paltrow): This one has a real late '90s rom-com sensibility to it tonally, which rubs some people the wrong way, but I think it's a delightfully timeless story of Emma's maturation, which is brought about by the good-natured truth telling of a friend (Northam as Mr. Knightly). This (good-natured truth telling of a friend) is a vibe we could probably use a lot more of in the church.

ROCKY MOVIE RUSHMORE

Rocky: This film won the Academy Award for Best Picture in 1976 and was the script, by Stallone, that launched the franchise and launched Stallone. This first one watches more like a little indie art film that is more about love and personal growth than it is about boxing. It's gritty, grimy, slow, heartfelt, and amazing. Also, Adrian's personal aesthetic in this movie may have "started" female hipsters, what with her Amish dresses, knitted beanies, and Lisa Loeb glasses that predated the real Lisa Loeb by like two decades.

Rocky IV: This one is also on my "movies that quantifiably suck but are fun to watch" Rushmore[*] in that it was made in 1985 and is very 1985—the whole thing is like one big montage involving steroids, mansions, Ferraris, a mean Russian, and ending the Cold War singlehandedly on Christmas Eve.

---

[*] *Top Gun* is also on this Rushmore.

Creed: This is the first movie in which Stallone allowed himself to be an old man (as opposed to a waxen, steroidal old man trying to look young), and it worked *really* well. He was endearing, sympathetic, and wise, and the boxing really looked good!

Rocky III: Mr. T is amazing as a would-be Mike Tyson figure (which is odd because this movie predated Tyson by a good five years), and the Rocky character deals with some real personal angst/growth in this one. It's also a great, grimy, 1980s Los Angeles movie.

WES ANDERSON RUSHMORE

Rushmore: This is a boys' boarding school movie that is, refreshingly, not set in New England. This movie started Bill Murray's run of playing burned-out, disaffected middle-aged men, which he is amazing at doing.

The Life Aquatic with Steve Zissou: This is more of Murray doing burned-out, disaffected, middle-aged-guy stuff, only this time doing it while being a past-it documentary filmmaker and doing it on a boat. This movie glamorizes boat stuff and wharf life, which you know I am here for.

The Royal Tenenbaums: Another great New York movie. I feel like this is the most "Wes Anderson" Wes movie and is delightful in that you get great performances out of both Wilson brothers, Murray, Gene Hackman, and Ben Stiller, who is really dialing it up in this one. Super fun.

Isle of Dogs: This is an animated movie about dogs—the plot of which is also, roughly, the plot of actual American life in 2020–2021 (it was released in 2018). Wild.

'90S MOVIE RUSHMORE

Good Will Hunting: This movie is *so* '90s in terms of both fashion and earnestness but is also absolutely elite from a dialogue and character standpoint. Also elite in terms of portraying realistic friendships between dudes of a certain age and in terms of being Robin Williams's best movie. I love it.

Singles: Cameron Crowe. Seattle.[*] Flannels. Coffee shops. Apartments. Guys starting bands. Angst.

Reality Bites: Ethan Hawke.[†] Houston.[‡] Apartments. Guys starting bands. Angst. Janeane Garofalo.

The Program: This is a terrible football movie that I watch annually and that is exceedingly '90s in terms of both tone and aesthetics. Also makes my "movies that glorify steroid use" Rushmore, along with *Rocky IV* and *Any Given Sunday.*

---

[*] Eddie Vedder, Jeff Ament, and Stone Gossard are in this too...which is awesome.

[†] Hawke plays a certain kind of greasy, arrogant-but-clearly-wildly-insecure philosophy-type kid *so well.* In this, he is Mr. '90s.

[‡] There aren't enough movies made in random, forgettable cities like Houston, Indianapolis, Charlotte, and Cincinnati. I'd be up for more in these random places.

APPENDIX B

ARE SPORTS DUMB? (A FRANK AND SELF-INDICTING DISCUSSION)

BY TED KLUCK AND BARNABAS PIPER

TK Near the end of the 3:30 block of NFL games yesterday, as Dallas Cowboys wide receiver CeeDee Lamb was peacocking into the end zone while taunting Jalen Mills, as middle-aged man Aaron Rodgers was indicating to the city of Chicago that he "[expletive] owns" them, as my beloved Detroit Lions (I know, I like pain) were getting donkeyed by yet another NFL opponent, and as I read about football coach Lane Kiffin being pelted with golf balls at the end of a college football game...I asked myself the very real question: Are sports dumb?

The coup de grâce—which the *Oxford Dictionary* defines as "a final blow or shot given to kill a wounded person or animal"—was my own personal NFL nemesis (due to a writing project gone horribly wrong) leading his team on an improbable game-winning drive in overtime. Granted, this one is a "me" problem, but still, I didn't think I'd have to see his face on television each weekend nearly a decade later. If my enemies are going to prosper, I'd rather not have to watch it.*

In some form or fashion, sports have been a part of my life—as a player, coach, or fan—for almost the entirety of it. And yet as I think of my own personal dumbest moments in life, many of them have to do with sports. The fact that this rather large correlation is just occurring to me is, itself, embarrassing.

Naturally, I put some hooks in the water via text.

"It took me until age 70 to learn that none of it matters," said my pops, who is an athlete, a fan, and also wise.

"Sports might *be* dumb, but they might also *attract* dumb," said my smart friend, who also likes sports.

"I don't know how not to care," said my son, who is in college, expressing a sentiment that I "get" at a very deep level.

Let's look at the examples from the opening paragraph again. CeeDee Lamb taunting his way into the end zone is dumb because no one in his industry has modeled how not to be dumb (or classy, let's say) in that particular way in a couple of decades. Simply put, he's just doing what he's seen modeled for him. The Lions losing isn't dumb, per se, but me caring about it or expecting anything from the Lions is, in fact, dumb. That one's on me. Aaron Rodgers declaring that he "owns" Chicago fans is probably just legitimately dumb behavior for a man of his age and stature and also dumb in light of probably having to play them again at some point. I don't know a lot of other men in their late thirties who act like this and then have seemingly no conscience about it afterward. The hubris is off the charts in that case, which (off-the-charts hubris) is almost always dumb.

In the case of my nemesis, me caring and me watching in hopes of the football universe delivering some shred of comeuppance or (for lack of a

---

* I know, I don't have to.

better term) "justice" on my behalf is just achingly dumb on my part and probably sinful. I'm embarrassed to admit it in print.

Also, the cutaway CBS shots of Jerry Jones (nearly 80 years old) hugging and jumping up and down in his luxury box after winning a football game hits at a dumb level to me, but it's hard to pinpoint why. Maybe I'd do the same thing? But I doubt it. Grown-ups throwing golf balls at other grown-ups is so dumb as to not even require explanation.

To that point, and I'm getting deep into the philosophical weeds here: Did anyone else catch a slight hint of "maybe this is dumb" vibes while watching Michael Jordan's iconic *The Last Dance* documentary? I mean, I love Jordan and I loved the doc, but still. Sacrificing friends, family, and almost every meaningful relationship in life to win at basketball...I dunno.

It's almost as though the legendary Vince Lombardi may have been wrong in indicating that winning is "the only thing." Dumbness, too, is very much a thing. And maybe I'm dumb for caring at all.

BP My initial instinct is to tell you that no, sports are *not* dumb. But I think that would primarily be self-justifying. I would mostly be saying that so I can feel good about the various temper tantrums I have thrown and TV remotes I have destroyed because of sports. (Thank you, Minnesota Vikings.) It would also be disingenuous and, I think, false to say that sports *are* definitively dumb.

As you so clearly pointed out, there is a huge amount of dumbness in sports. But is it more than any other part of life? We can turn anything dumb, even good stuff. We just wrote chapters upon chapters about Christian fame and Christian conferences and over-the-top holiday traditions, for goodness' sake. We can make church dumb and pastoring dumb and worship music dumb and even Christmas dumb. Dumb is our default, I think.

What I'm getting at is that sports are not dumb, but we can inject them with it. We bring ego and insecurity and a gaping void in our hearts to sports just like we do to love and work and parenting and everything else. And that's when we turn our children's T-ball game into a résumé builder or a beautiful fall afternoon at Neyland Stadium into a beer-soaked, golf ball–chucking rage fest. (As an aside and as a fellow transplant to Tennessee, is it a local tradition to bring golf balls to a college football game? I get throwing beer cans or sodas or something. But golf balls?)

Sports are awesome, and I know you agree with me. We've both learned so much about hard work, failure, teamwork, leadership, competition, and humility (and humiliation), and we've had a plain old good time doing so. We love to watch sports with friends and family, soak up the atmosphere at a minor league ballpark, and jump out of our seats to cheer for a breakaway dunk or a long TD. We've developed real, meaningful friendships through sports and had the chance to influence the lives of others through coaching. So no, sports aren't dumb. We are sometimes, and that can foul up an otherwise fantastic pastime.

TK No, man, you're absolutely right, and that's an important distinction. The "dumb" parts (read: sin nature) reside squarely in our own hearts, and that's on us. And yet we're continually drawn to sports for their ability to deliver something magical—a moment, a relationship, a memory.

Sports is the ultimate high-ceiling, low-floor endeavor in that many of my happiest and most hopeful moments in life have come from sports. Some of my fondest memories of childhood involve falling asleep in the passenger's seat of my dad's car as we drove home from some stadium or arena late at night, stopping to get sodas and roast beef sandwiches at some random gas station that had a good deli. The fact that we got to see Dan Marino, Jerry Rice, Eric Dickerson, Tony Mandarich, and so many other greats in their primes is part of the magic too and creates a lifelong cache of memories that bond us together.

Just the other day, I got an out-of-the-blue text from one of my former long snappers at Lane College, where I coach. The text simply said "I miss you guys" and was accompanied by an award-quality photo of me standing next to our punter, chatting on the sideline before the game. It was a moment frozen in time, on a day full of many moments, but it delighted me that he cared enough to send it and to remember similar times and similar chats we'd had on sidelines together.

That's the magic of sports.

To learn more about Harvest House books and
to read sample chapters, visit our website:

www.harvesthousepublishers.com

HARVEST HOUSE PUBLISHERS
EUGENE, OREGON